AF235216

TEACHER HACKS

HISTORY

BY

REBECCA CHADWICK

SERIES EDITOR: MICHAEL CHILES

Together we unlock every learner's unique potential

At Hachette Learning (formerly Hodder Education), there's one thing we're certain about. No two students learn the same way. That's why our approach to teaching begins by recognising the needs of individuals first.

Our mission is to allow every learner to fulfil their unique potential by empowering those who teach them. From our expert teaching and learning resources to our digital educational tools that make learning easier and more accessible for all, we provide solutions designed to maximise the impact of learning for every teacher, parent and student.

Aligned to our parent company, Hachette Livre, founded in 1826, we pride ourselves on being a learning solutions provider with a global footprint.

www.hachettelearning.com

Although every effort has been made to ensure that website addresses are correct at time of going to press, Hachette Learning cannot be held responsible for the content of any website mentioned in this book. It is sometimes possible to find a relocated web page by typing in the address of the home page for a website in the URL window of your browser.

Hachette UK's policy is to use papers that are natural, renewable and recyclable products and made from wood grown in well-managed forests and other controlled sources. The logging and manufacturing processes are expected to conform to the environmental regulations of the country of origin.

To order, please visit www.HachetteLearning.com or contact Customer Service at education@hachette.co.uk / +44 (0)1235 827827.

ISBN: 978 1 0360 0623 5

© Rebecca Chadwick 2026

First published in 2026 by
Hachette Learning (a trading division of Hodder and Stoughton Limited),
An Hachette UK Company
Carmelite House
50 Victoria Embankment
London EC4Y 0DZ
www.HachetteLearning.com

The authorised representative in the EEA is Hachette Ireland, 8 Castlecourt Centre, Dublin 15, D15 XTP3, Ireland (email: info@hbgi.ie)

Impression number   10 9 8 7 6 5 4 3 2 1
Year   2030 2029 2028 2027 2026

All rights reserved. Apart from any use permitted under UK copyright law, no part of this publication may be reproduced or transmitted in any form or by any means, electronic or mechanical, including photocopying and recording, or held within any information storage and retrieval system, without permission in writing from the publisher or under licence from the Copyright Licensing Agency Limited. Further details of such licences (for reprographic reproduction) may be obtained from the Copyright Licensing Agency Limited, www.cla.co.uk

Cover photo
Typeset in the UK.
Printed in the UK.

A catalogue record for this title is available from the British Library.

MIX
Paper | Supporting responsible forestry
FSC
www.fsc.org
FSC™ C104740

ABOUT THE AUTHOR

Rebecca has been teaching for ten years in a range of settings. She has also had the opportunity to present at Research Ed and contribute to case studies in exam series.

Working as a team leader for both AQA and Edexcel she has been able to support schools with their delivery of GCSE qualifications.

With a passion for reading, running and tackling the Wainwrights at the weekend you will normally find her outdoors.

TABLE OF CONTENTS

FOREWORD

Teaching is complex, and the cognitive demands are substantial. Teachers are seen as masters of their subject from day 1, but teaching requires 'in the moment' decisions to be made when knowledge and understanding of the intricacies of curriculum design may be imperfect. Teachers need to learn on the job to quickly develop an understanding of the most effective approaches to teaching, and skilfully use these approaches to deliver subject matter to their students in a way that they will understand.

In recent years, schools have invested a lot of time and thought into how we can codify teaching pedagogy so that it creates consistency, clarity and a shared understanding among teachers. By establishing clear, research-informed methods for instruction, schools can ensure that teachers know and can apply effective practices that are easily replicable and adaptable, and that can contribute towards maintaining high standards across diverse classrooms and curriculums. However, despite all the research, we still grapple with views on the best pedagogy approaches, and this can make continuing professional development (CPD) somewhat confusing.

One area of professional development that does not seem to get the same limelight is subject pedagogy development. We often assume that once a teacher is qualified, they can automatically teach their subject. However, the role of subject pedagogy professional development in schools is a crucial part to support teaching and learning, as it contributes towards the unique demands of each subject in the curriculum. Effective subject-specific pedagogy enables teachers to break down complex concepts into more-accessible steps, making it easier for students to grasp challenging material.

In this book, Rebecca provides a comprehensive guide on how to approach the teaching of history in schools. From chronology and causation to disciplinary thinking and historical enquiry, this book provides detailed guidance on how you might approach teaching these elements in your classroom.

The aim of this book, as with all the books in the Teacher Hacks series, is to provide an insight into a teacher's classroom; a look through the keyhole to see how expert practitioners approach some of the most complex and challenging elements of their subject. In this book, this is exactly what Rebecca has done. Rebecca uses her experience to highlight the challenges of teaching history and shares some of her teaching hacks to help others in their classrooms.

Michael Chiles

INTRODUCTION

Fixing the plane mid-flight: The reality of teaching history

A history teacher's job is never truly finished. Just as we think we've nailed a sequence or finally feel secure in a topic, a new Prime Minister is elected, a fresh historical documentary reinterprets the past, an international conflict breaks out or another curriculum review rolls around. The past might be fixed, but our understanding of it – and how we teach it – is in constant motion.

It's a job that requires you to keep one foot in the archives and the other in the here and now. New leaders, cabinet reshuffles, economic shifts, global crises and emerging scholarship are always demanding our attention. History doesn't sit still, and neither does the history teacher. That can be exciting but, if we're honest, it can also feel utterly exhausting.

There are questions I ask myself at least once a week (if not daily): Is my curriculum diverse and inclusive enough? Are students encountering voices that have been historically marginalised? What are the foundational skills I need them to develop – and how do I teach those at key stage 3 without reducing everything to an exam rehearsal? How do I ensure they're equipped to write analytically, evaluate interpretations and engage critically with the past? Am I preparing them for life beyond the exam, as well as the exam itself? And while I'm juggling all of that, how do I stay up to date with pedagogy, research and the ever-expanding list of must-read historical texts?

Trying to answer all these questions simultaneously can feel like trying to fix a plane mid-flight – the engine's rattling, a wing needs tightening, and someone in row 6 still doesn't understand how to use the seatbelt. It's hectic. It's relentless. But somehow, we keep flying. This image is taken from Dylan Wiliam's (2011) work on formative assessment but has stuck with me as a metaphor for teaching.

And in spite of it all, I truly believe this is one of the greatest jobs in the world.

This book isn't a step-by-step manual or a claim to perfection. I'm not suggesting I have all the answers. What I do have are hard-earned insights, honest reflections and a decade's worth of lessons learned in the classroom – the successes, the near misses and the occasional facepalm moments that led to growth. Some of these strategies have transformed how I teach. Others started with great promise and ended up on the metaphorical scrapheap – but even those were worth trying.

My aim is to offer a collection of practical, teacher-tested hacks to make the job a little smoother and maybe even more joyful. They're grounded in research but shaped by real classroom experience. Some will help you sharpen your curriculum or make your questioning more purposeful. Others are about saving time, reducing workload or simply getting through the week with a little less stress.

This book is for:

- New teachers wondering how on earth to get started without drowning in content.
- Mid-career teachers trying to juggle increasing responsibility with their love for the subject.
- Experienced teachers looking to tweak, refine or just feel reinspired.

If you've ever spent your Sunday night planning a lesson you thought would last an hour but barely filled 25 minutes, if you've ever had a Year 9 class ask whether Henry VIII was alive during World War I or if you've ever made a lesson plan so good that you wished you were in your own class – this is for you.

So let's embrace the chaos, celebrate the creativity, and share what works. Not to chase perfection, but to make the job just that bit more doable – and maybe, along the way, remind ourselves why we chose to teach history in the first place.

Because while we may not be able to fix the whole plane mid-air, we can definitely keep it flying – and maybe even enjoy the view while we're up there.

Rebecca Chadwick

CHAPTER 1:
TEACHING CHRONOLOGY –
BUILDING THE BACKBONE
OF THE PAST

Chronology is the history teacher's staple. To borrow from the Historical Association, it's the "air history breathes." And rightly so – a limited understanding of chronology inevitably leads to a limited understanding of history itself. Students need to be able to place what they are learning into a bigger picture of the past. That means more than knowing dates or rulers. It means understanding how events connect, influence each other and evolve across time. It's about threads, not snapshots.

I'll admit, I've often found myself mid-lesson, utterly engrossed in painting the narrative links between topics. My inner *Dead Poets Society* moment. Sweeping gestures. Passionate storytelling. Arms waving, voice rising, eyes sparkling as I lay out the grand sweep of history, connecting one event to another across centuries. In my head, I'm inspiring a room full of budding historians, lighting intellectual fires that will burn long into adulthood. I'm imagining them going home, digging out old history books, passionately debating over dinner, researching revolutions by choice.

In reality? They're probably wondering what's for lunch. Or how long until the bell. Or whether they remembered their PE kit. And you know what? That's fair.

Because unless we make chronology a visible, deliberate part of every student's learning journey – not just a one-off timeline lesson or the occasional reference to "the last topic" – students won't see those connections automatically. They don't arrive with a ready-made mental map of the past. That map has to be built, brick by brick, thread by thread, through careful sequencing, constant reinforcement and explicit reference to what came before and what comes next.

The danger is that, without this, history becomes a collection of isolated events: Tudors one term, World War I the next. And to students, it can all seem disconnected. As though Henry VIII and trench warfare happened in completely separate universes – not along the same winding timeline.

So the real question becomes: how do we bring the importance of chronology to life without sacrificing 20 minutes of every lesson to narrative exposition? How do we build that bigger picture in a way that sticks, that students can access and return to and that helps them build meaningful, conceptual links across time?

Because when students do start to grasp chronology – when they begin to see how events flow, collide, echo and evolve – that's when history becomes not just content, but a living, breathing way of thinking about the world. And that's where the magic really happens.

Why chronology matters

Chronological understanding isn't about memorising dates. It's not about rattling off monarchs or listing every battle in order. What it really does is enable students to:

- Track change and continuity over time.
- Locate interpretations and sources in their appropriate context.
- Develop analytical frameworks to compare periods and evaluate significance.

Chronology gives students a structure – a skeleton to hang everything else on. Without it, historical knowledge becomes unanchored. Students can recall isolated facts or stories, but they don't always know how they fit together. One minute they're learning about medieval kings, the next, they're looking at Cold War politics, and it all feels like jumping from channel to channel on a television without any idea of what came before.

And that's where the misconceptions creep in.

I've lost count of how many times I've heard students say something like, "Wasn't Hitler fighting in World War II and World War I at the same time?" or "Did the Romans come after the Victorians?" They know certain names and events, but without a secure chronological framework, the timeline becomes blurred. They remember that Hitler was a soldier in World War I and a dictator in World War II, but can't quite figure out how one led to the other. They've heard of the Industrial Revolution, but might think it happened after World War I simply because that's the order they learned them in.

That's the crux of the issue: teaching history in order isn't enough. I used to think it was. My logic was, "Year 7: start with the Normans. Year 8: early modern. Year 9: the modern world. Sorted!"

Voila! Chronology!

Except it really doesn't work that way.

Because unless we teach chronology as a conceptual structure, rather than a simple sequence, students won't naturally build those connections. They need help understanding why the English Reformation matters to their later study of empire. They need to see how industrialisation created the conditions for both urban reform and global conflict. And they need repeated opportunities to practise linking events across time, not just within a single topic.

What I've learned – often the hard way – is that chronology isn't a box to tick at the start of Year 7. It's something to be returned to, revisited and re-anchored at every stage of the journey. It's the golden thread that holds the curriculum together, and the map that students need to navigate the complex terrain of the past.

So if we want students to think historically – to compare, analyse and evaluate with confidence – we have to help them build that chronological framework step by step. Otherwise, they're just collecting puzzle pieces without ever seeing the full picture.

Before planning a lesson or unit, consider:

- What's the main aim of this scheme of work? How does it sit within the wider curriculum?
- What prior knowledge do students need to access this lesson?
- Are there any chronological jumps between topics or half terms? How can I bridge them?
- What is the mathematical fluency of the class? Can they confidently calculate intervals or place decades in order?

HACK #1

Do Nows / starters that connect: A well-structured Do Now or starter can do heavy lifting in building chronological awareness.

In practice

For example, before beginning a unit on World War I, I set retrieval questions linked to the Empire and Industrial Revolution units previously studied:

- List three countries colonised under the British Empire.
- Why did the British expand their empire?
- When was the Industrial Revolution?
- Where did most people work during this period?

These questions aren't flashy – but they're deliberate. They help students retrieve contextual knowledge, spark connections and prepare their brains for the historical moment they're about to enter.

The impact is immediate. Within minutes of starting the World War I unit, students are already drawing links: "So that is because of..." or "That connects to when..." If they don't make these connections themselves, some questioning will guide them towards this. Taking the time to plan these questions with the chronology of the lesson or scheme of work in mind will make these purposeful and impactful.

HACK #2

Road maps and learning journeys: Students need to know where they are going – and where they've come from – in terms of their curriculum journey. I use visual road maps or simplified timelines at the start of a topic, sometimes scaled to the scheme, sometimes showing the full year. This can be as simple as three images:

- Last topic (e.g. the Atomic Bomb).
- This lesson (e.g. Churchill's Iron Curtain speech).
- Next topic (e.g. the Truman Doctrine).

Used consistently, these become powerful cognitive anchors. Students form mental models through repeated visual cues. It's manageable. It's meaningful. And it supports recall and sequencing for GCSE account questions.

As Sydney Wood (1995) put it, "The past is chaotic to pupils, until sequenced." Just don't show the entire timeline at once. It overwhelms. Three steps is enough to keep it focused.

In practice

At the start of the lesson, every lesson, we talk through this road map for the learning cycle (half term) of lessons, showing students connections and making links to any previous topics or years of learning. This way students are able to see both the skills and coherence of the curriculum in action. They can then use these road maps as revision tools at the end of the learning cycle to annotate key retrieval.

HACK #3

Meanwhile, elsewhere: The breadth of key stage 3 is enough to give any department lead sleepless nights. Eighteen (if you're lucky) units to cover the history of the world? Piece of cake, right? The reality is more complex. Some difficult choices have to be made of what to include, meaning that there are some jumps within this chronology, ways to bridge this gap can become difficult.

In practice

A simple but effective solution: use Meanwhile, elsewhere tasks as homework. While studying the English Civil War, set a task exploring what was happening in Mughal India at the same time. It's not about depth, it's about perspective. This allows students to make the connections not only across chronology but also different countries and locations, ensuring that they see beyond themselves.

I've found that students become curious. They ask how their homework links to the core topic. Some dig deeper independently. That spark of curiosity is exactly what we're aiming for.

HACK #4

Synoptic threads and conceptual links: Chronology becomes clearer when students revisit recurring themes: empire, migration, trade, power, warfare.

In practice

Use these as throughlines:

- Where have we seen this before?
- How has warfare changed over time?
- What's similar about these empires?

Use these prompts in starters or Do Nows to build their synoptic thinking. It pays dividends in Period Studies at GCSE, where thematic thinking is essential.

Final thought

Chronology isn't a bolt-on. It's the structure that holds the subject together. Without it, we're just teaching disconnected stories. With it, students start to understand how events build on one another, how the world changes and how the past still shapes the present.

This chapter is just the beginning. Chronology will weave through many of the hacks in this book – because building the big picture is what gives history its meaning.

CASE STUDY:
JOHN HOUGH – SEQUENCING

I've been thinking recently about some of the "big ideas" of cognitive science and how they play out in conversations between history teachers, especially sequencing and prior learning. I think they're reduced to the order we teach stuff in (typically chronologically) and getting kids to remember things at the start of the lesson.

A quick win has been to recognise where the sequencing starts specifically for meaning making, which is usually long before we think, instead of speaking of sequencing in terms of years/terms/half terms.

I've been wrapping this around the idea of accessibility – a term that we used to use a lot in teaching but sort of lost somewhere along the way. I think it helps us shift our thinking for the better and is fairly quick to implement. For example, it could be exemplified through the Black Death (a deceptively tricky topic that gets lost in remembering symptoms and learning from sources).

We want pupils to be able to analyse and assess the impact of the Black Death on society. One of these categories might be the psychological trauma of loss and grief but how accessible is this idea if thinking of our Black Death sequence starts in 1348? Pupils cannot access the trauma of mass graves, no last rites, no precessions of loved ones and neighbours, no available priest without first studying what a "good death" meant to deeply religious medieval people before the Black Death.

I think this is beautifully presented in John Hatcher's story of Walsham. There are so many ideas contained within the first few chapters, all before the Black Death, that make it accessible for readers. In terms of a case study, it would be something like "using rich encounters to make ideas in history accessible," highlighting the importance of story and showing that pieces of scholarship have often done the thinking for us as curriculum designers.

CHAPTER 2: TEACHING CAUSATION – THE DOMINOES OF HISTORY

Causation is one of those historical concepts that sounds simple – until you try to teach it. It's the question that sits at the heart of the discipline: Why did this happen? But that "why" is a tangle of human decisions, chance, structure and consequence.

Causation, in the simplest terms, is the idea that every event or development was influenced by something that came before. Yet that definition barely scratches the surface. History rarely works like a neat equation where X leads directly to Y. It's closer to a web – full of overlapping threads, unintended consequences and competing interpretations.

I learned this the hard way. In my first few years teaching, I'd find myself giving students the same explanation for every major event: "This happened because of..." followed by a list of causes. It felt neat. It was logical. But when I read their essays, every cause carried the same weight, every paragraph ended with "this was a cause of..." and I realised I hadn't taught them causation at all – I'd taught them description.

Understanding causation requires chronological awareness, yes, but also a sense of connection and contingency. It's what allows students to move from reciting facts to analysing forces. To ask not only what happened, but why, how and whether it could have been different.

Causation is also the gateway to debate – the point where historical thinking becomes argumentative. When a student can weigh the importance of economic, political and social causes, they're doing what historians do: interpreting the past through evidence.

But teaching this skill takes time, structure and a lot of modelling. Over the years, I've built a set of hacks that help students move beyond "one cause, one consequence" thinking and into the rich, layered understanding that history deserves.

Understanding causation is often where students begin to truly think like historians. But because it requires weighing, comparing and linking ideas, it's not always intuitive – especially for younger or less confident learners. Below are several practical approaches I've used to make causation accessible, engaging and rigorous.

HACK #1

Make causation concrete: Abstract thinking is hard for many students, so start with the tangible. Before tackling the causes of World War I, I build a row of dominoes. We tip the first one, and students watch the chain reaction unfold. Then I ask: "Which domino mattered most?"

In that moment, causation stops being theoretical. We can talk about the "trigger" (the assassination of Archduke Franz Ferdinand) versus the "underlying causes" (militarism, alliances, imperialism, nationalism – the classic Main framework). Students immediately grasp that not every cause carries equal weight.

To make this stick, I sometimes give them scenarios outside of history – "Why did you come to school late today?" The answers range from "my alarm didn't go off" to "my mum was stuck in traffic." They see how multiple causes can operate simultaneously.

In practice
- Use metaphor and modelling. Physical demonstrations like dominoes, Jenga towers or branching flowcharts turn abstract relationships into visible thinking.
- Return to these metaphors often – especially when revisiting topics across time. Students will begin to transfer the logic of causal thinking from one unit to another.

HACK #2

Layer, don't list: When students first attempt causation essays, they tend to list: "One cause was...Another cause was..." and so on. The challenge is helping them connect causes – to see interplay and hierarchy.

In practice

I model this by using causal webs rather than bullet points. We start by categorising causes (political, economic, social, religious), then use arrows to show links between them. For example:

"The Industrial Revolution (economic) → increased urbanisation (social), which → intensified demands for reform (political)."

Each arrow is an opportunity for a connective phrase: "as a result", "this led to", "consequently", "therefore".

Over time, I fade the scaffold – moving from webs to paragraphs – but the structure remains in their reasoning. Moving into plenary tasks from the *Writing Revolution* such as "because, but" and "so, also" help to get students to consider the impact of different events in the unit – how does one lead to the next?

The theory

Counsell (2018) and Fordham (2016) stress that historical reasoning develops through understanding how causes interact. Students need to see causal networks, not isolated triggers. Structuring this visually reduces cognitive load (Sweller, 1988) and builds fluency in analysis.

HACK #3

The challenge and the solution: Causation brings predictable stumbling blocks – so I teach the challenges alongside the strategies to overcome them.

Challenge	Solution
Students treat all causes as equal.	Teach significance ranking. "Which cause had the biggest impact, and why?" Use Diamond Nine activities to order importance. Then model writing with comparative connectives: "Although nationalism was significant, militarism created the conditions for war."
Students conflate cause and consequence.	Use explicit dual columns during planning – one for causes, one for effects – and build transition sentences: "This caused…which in turn led to…"
Students see causation as linear, not complex.	Introduce cyclical models (feedback loops). For instance, "Industrial growth caused urbanisation, which increased demand for further industrial growth."
Students forget chronology.	Integrate retrieval questions that anchor causes in time: "Which came first – the introduction of conscription or the alliance with France?" Repetition embeds sequencing.

 **HACK #4**

Use the language of analysis early: One of the best ways to build causal reasoning is through language. I introduce evaluative phrases as early as Year 7. "The most important reason was...", "A short-term trigger was...", "A long-term cause might have been...".

By embedding this vocabulary from the start, students develop the language of judgement – a skill that pays dividends at GCSE and A-level.

In practice

After analysing the Peasants' Revolt, I ask:

- "Which cause mattered most?"
- "Was it short-term or long-term?"
- "Could the revolt have been avoided?"

Each question pushes them toward analytical reasoning rather than descriptive recall.

 HACK #5

Connect across time: Causation isn't limited to individual events. Once students grasp the skill, use it to draw connections across eras. For example:

- "How did the causes of World War I compare to the causes of World War II?"
- "How did industrialisation in the 18th century shape empire in the 19th?"

These synoptic comparisons strengthen schema and build the big picture understanding that underpins historical literacy (Counsell and Burn, 2016).

Final thought

Teaching causation is teaching thinking. It's what moves students from memorising to reasoning, from seeing history as a series of accidents to understanding it as a series of choices, contexts and consequences.

There's something magical about that moment when a student says, "So the assassination didn't cause the war – it just lit the fuse." You can almost hear their mental model shift.

Helping them reach that point is the essence of our job – not just teaching what happened, but showing how history itself happens.

CHAPTER 3: SOURCE ANALYSIS – SEEING THROUGH THE HISTORIAN'S LENS

Source analysis is the heartbeat of history teaching. It's one of the most authentic ways for students to engage with the discipline – to think, question and interpret like historians.

But it's also one of the trickiest skills to teach. Even after years in the classroom, I still find myself tweaking and refining how I introduce, model and assess source work. There's something wonderfully unpredictable about how students approach sources: one will produce a perceptive insight that makes you beam, another will write, "This source is biased" as though that alone solves everything.

Over the years, I've learned that source analysis is less about clever acronyms and more about nurturing curiosity, scepticism and methodical reasoning. It's about helping students understand that sources are not just windows into the past – they're voices from it.

Whether it's a 17th-century woodcut, a soldier's letter from the trenches or a Cold War propaganda poster, sources give us the texture of human experience. But they also demand that we ask awkward questions. Who created this? Why? What's missing? What might we not see?

Why source analysis is hard – and why that's okay

Wineburg (2001) famously described sourcing as an "unnatural act". And he wasn't wrong. He found that expert historians approach sources differently to novices. They begin by interrogating the origin – who wrote this, when and why? They contextualise, thinking about the broader moment in time. And they corroborate, weighing one piece of evidence against others. Students, on the other hand, often default to literary analysis. They read the source like a poem or novel – drawing meaning from the words, but rarely questioning who created them or what they were trying to achieve.

That's not a criticism – it's a cognitive habit. In English, students are taught to extract meaning and symbolism from every phrase. But in history, we're not just asking, "What does this say?" We're asking, "Why does it say that?" "What does it not say?" "And how does that affect its value as evidence?" That leap – from content to context to consequence – is huge.

Christodoulou (2017) echoes this view. She argues that source analysis places huge demands on working memory. Students must decode unfamiliar vocabulary, make sense of the content, consider the historical context, analyse the provenance and then bring in their own prior knowledge – often within the space of a single question. When students struggle, it's rarely a sign of laziness. More often, it's because the task itself hasn't been made clear or accessible.

We've all seen students freeze mid-sentence when writing about a source – not because they don't know what it says, but because they don't know what to do with it. They might fixate on an irrelevant detail or fall back on generic claims: "This is biased because it's a cartoon," or "This source is reliable because it's from the time." These are not analytical conclusions. They're survival strategies, attempts to sound right when students aren't quite sure what the question is really asking.

It's easy to reach for acronyms like PETAL or PEE. They promise structure. They offer something neat. But, more often than not, they reduce source work to formula. They teach students how to write, but not how to think.

So rather than overwhelming our students with content-heavy sources and hoping they spot the significance, we need to provide a scaffolded, sequenced approach. That means modelling the thinking out loud. It means starting with what they can see, then helping them to layer in meaning. It means giving them the vocabulary to express uncertainty, the confidence to make tentative judgements and the opportunity to grapple with conflicting interpretations.

We might begin by simply asking: "What do you notice?" Then, "What might that suggest?" And only later, "What does this mean in light of the question?" When students realise that, while not every source has a hidden trick to uncover, rather they all have a voice to understand, their approach begins to shift.

It's not quick. It's not easy. But it's what makes the history classroom a place of genuine enquiry – where students don't just learn about the past, they learn how to question it.

HACK #1

Starting with what they see: One of the best changes I made in my teaching practice was learning to slow down the introduction of a source. If we want students to analyse deeply, we need to create the space for them to actually notice things.

In practice
I now start with a simple – but surprisingly powerful – routine:

- What can you see?
- What does this suggest?
- What do you know?

This three-question model gives students a manageable structure to start with. It also helps them build a bridge from the source to their wider historical understanding. For image sources especially, this approach creates a natural entry point – even for less confident learners.

HACK #2

The drawing game: If classroom culture allows, I'll start with one of my favourite starters, a light-hearted but effective exercise. One student turns their back to the screen. The other has to describe the image in as much detail as possible for their partner to draw. Cue laughter, wildly inaccurate interpretations – and some fascinating conversations. "Why did you describe that part first?" "What did you miss?" We then revisit the source together with fresh eyes and much more attention to detail.

It might seem playful, but this activity builds habits of close observation and challenges assumptions – something historians do all the time.

 **HACK #3**

Beyond bias – building better language: Too often, student source analysis gets stuck at "this is biased" or "this is reliable because it's a first-hand account." That's not analysis, it's regurgitation. So how do we move them forward?

First, we teach the language of uncertainty. Wiltshire (2000) and Le Cocq (2000) both stress that students need subject-specific language to express tentative conclusions: terms like "perhaps", "suggests", "may imply", "could reflect", "limited by...". These don't weaken historical writing – they strengthen it by showing nuance and awareness of perspective.

We also need to unpick provenance explicitly. I've had success breaking this down into:

- Who produced the source?
- When was it produced?
- Why was it produced?
- Who was it intended for?

Once students get into the habit of answering these four questions every time, their ability to write meaningfully about provenance improves dramatically. I don't ask for it all at once in early key stage 3 – but by key stage 4, students should be able to fold that analysis into the wider context and use it to assess utility and reliability.

 HACK #4

Using multiple choice to promote thinking: Christodoulou (2017) also advocates using multiple choice questions to develop inference and close reading. Not the tick-the-box kind, but well-crafted, nuanced MCQs where several options could *technically* be true, but only one is best supported by the source.

For example:

What is the main message of this source?
A. That the government was very effective during this period.
B. That public morale was low due to rationing.
C. That propaganda was used to boost national pride.
D. That British citizens supported the war effort.

Students have to justify their choice using evidence from the source and prior knowledge. The discussion that follows is often more valuable than any written answer.

 HACK #5

Reducing cognitive load, one layer at a time: According to Sweller's (1988) cognitive load theory, students learn best when we reduce extraneous demands on their working memory. This applies powerfully to source analysis. If we throw a complex cartoon and a GCSE-style question at students simultaneously, we're almost guaranteed to lose some of them – if not in body, then certainly in focus.

In practice

So we break it down.

1. First, analyse content: What is this showing or saying?
2. Then, discuss context: When was this made, and what was happening at the time?
3. Then, explore provenance: Who made it and why?
4. Then, link to knowledge: What do we know that helps us understand this better?
5. Finally, evaluate significance or utility: How useful is it for answering the historical question?

This step-by-step process helps all learners – especially those who struggle with literacy – to access what is often the most cognitively demanding part of the lesson.

HACK #6

Story-source-scholarship – a shortcut without shortcuts: One of my favourite routines for source analysis – especially when time is tight – is what I call the story-source-scholarship model. Here's how it works:

- **Story:** Start with a short narrative about an event or period. Keep it readable, accessible and, ideally, human-focused.
- **Source:** Present a contemporary source linked to that story. Guide students through analysis.
- **Scholarship:** Introduce a historian's interpretation. How has the event been interpreted over time?

This format allows you to explore context, content and change in interpretation – all in one lesson. It also reinforces the idea that sources are not just clues to "what happened" – they're part of the construction of history.

Quick hacks that make a big difference

- Source booklets: Collect sources across a unit in one place. Add space for annotation and link each source to enquiry questions.
- Key phrases prompt sheet: Build a bank of helpful language:"This suggests…","This source was created to…","Given the context, this implies…".
- Mini whiteboards: Great for quick inference practice. Display a source and ask: "What does this detail suggest?" All students respond at once – immediate feedback, maximum engagement.

Final thought

Source analysis is the historian's heartbeat – a rhythm of questioning, reading, and re-evaluating, and a form of historical empathy. It's also one of the most rewarding parts of teaching history, because it's where students begin to see that the past isn't fixed.

They learn that history is constructed – debated, contested, human.

There's a moment that stays with me every year: a student frowning at a propaganda poster and saying, "So…this isn't really true, is it?"

That spark – that realisation that truth and evidence are separate things – is when you know they're not just learning history. They're learning to think historically.

CHAPTER 4: TEACHING WRITING – TURNING THOUGHT INTO ARGUMENT

"All teachers are teachers of literacy."

It's a phrase we hear often. But for history teachers, this responsibility takes on another level of complexity. With exam questions demanding fully developed arguments, engagement with sources and sophisticated essay structures, history isn't just close to English – it often mirrors it. I've had conversations with our brilliant English department where we compare exam papers and shake our heads at just how alike the demands are.

Whether we like it or not, writing essays is an integral part of being a history teacher. But I'll be honest – this is something I haven't always got right. Finding the balance between content and writing skills is tough. I often tell my students that history is a tricky juggling act: we're working with challenging content and difficult skills. Sometimes the balls drop. That's okay. What matters is creating systems that help us juggle better.

Working with exam boards has helped sharpen my understanding of what exam questions are really asking. But trying to embed those expectations into the classroom – often with less curriculum time than English – has taken time, trial and a lot of learning. Over the past two years, I've developed a series of strategies that have improved and, crucially, streamlined how we teach writing in history.

HACK #1

A consistent approach to writing: Wrigglesworth and McKeever (2010) argue that students need to know exactly what they're expected to write, why they're writing it and how it should be structured. As teachers, we've all faced the relentless "But why?" questions – and writing is no different. Clarity is everything.

Dylan Wiliam's (2011) work on formative assessment helped me reframe my approach. He emphasises the importance of clarifying success criteria and modelling the steps of a task. I also leaned on Harry Fletcher-Wood's (2018) work on redrafting and Wiliam's brilliant coaching analogy: that we wouldn't just ask a student to "throw a ball better" without breaking down the technique. Why do we expect any different in writing?

This was the mindset shift. I began focusing on the process of writing, not just the final product.

At ResearchED Warrington, I shared this journey under the title "Bringing the Goalposts Closer". The idea is rooted in evidence: self-regulated learning (SRL) is one of the most effective ways to improve outcomes (Hattie, 2013; Zimmerman and Bandura, 1994). But students can't self-regulate what they don't understand. They need both explicit instruction and low-stakes practice.

I've wrestled with this as a teacher. Like many of you, I have doubts about high-stakes exams. But if we're preparing students for them, we owe it to them to demystify the process.

HACK #2

Building self-regulated writers: To support self-regulated learning in writing:

- Clarify each step in the process of constructing an answer.
- Normalise error and uncertainty as part of the journey.
- Create risk-free spaces to practise writing.
- Personalise goals for students. For some, it's writing a dynamic opening sentence. For others, it's developing more layered analysis.

According to Pintrich (2000), self-regulated learners set goals, reflect on their outcomes and adjust their strategies accordingly. Our role is to structure this process without removing challenge.

HACK #3

Our department's writing structure: To build consistency, our department reviewed all our written tasks and exam-style questions across key stages 3 and 4. We looked for patterns and overlaps – not to create a rigid formula, but to ensure shared language and structure.

The outcome was a four-step success criteria we now use across every written task. Not a frame. Not a scaffold. A flexible structure that can grow with the student.

Success Criteria 1: Dynamic Opening Sentence (DOS)

This is where it begins. The DOS should answer the question directly and confidently in the very first line. We encourage students to remove the rest of the paragraph and ask: if all I wrote was the first sentence, did I still answer the question?

We deliberately moved away from PEEL structures, which often prioritise shape over substance. This shift to a dynamic approach gives clarity and direction from the outset.

Success Criteria 2: Evidence

Here comes the history. The evidence must support the DOS clearly and specifically.

We introduced the acronym SPED (Statistics, People, Events, Dates) to help students articulate what "evidence" actually means. It's not about listing facts. It's about selecting meaningful knowledge.

For source or interpretation questions, this evidence is drawn from the material itself – a quote, a description of an image. Whatever the task, Success Criteria 2 is always about evidence.

Success Criteria 3: Explanation

The hardest part. This is where students say: "So what?"

How does the evidence help answer the question? What does it mean? Why is it significant?

For students with weaker literacy, this can be the sticking point. Often, I've given students the target to explain but not really clarified or modelled what this means. That's why we anchor this step with a phrase in modelling: "This meant that..." It's a useful launchpad that can be developed into more ambitious writing as students gain confidence.

In source work, this explanation links knowledge with interpretation, showing how understanding supports or unpacks what is shown.

We've started to use structure strips to support this, asking questions that guide the students towards this explanatory thinking. So, for example, with the 16 mark Cold War question for AQA, we base our explanation on three key questions. How did the USA react? How did the USSR react? How did the world react? These consistent questions get students to consider the impact of the evidence that they are using.

Success Criteria 4: Analysis

Finally, students are asked to make a mini judgement. This is the flourish at the end of the paragraph that elevates a response.

Depending on the question, it might involve:

- Judging significance (e.g., long-term vs short-term impact)
- Commenting on utility (e.g., how helpful the source is)
- Returning to the line of argument.

Making it stick: Language, not frame

The key to this structure is not the criteria itself – it's the shared language. Every teacher in the department uses these terms. Every student hears them repeatedly.

We embed it into our feedback. We reference it in modelling. We celebrate when it's used well. It's not a rigid template – it's a guide.

Wiliam (2011) warns against writing frames that become crutches. Too often, I see exam scripts where the structure is scrawled at the top, but never used. True writing support must teach how arguments are built, not just how they're shaped.

By building a writing process that fits our students, our subject and our context, we give students the best chance at success – not just in exams, but as confident, independent historians.

Writing in history is hard. But it's also one of the most rewarding skills we can teach. When students start answering questions with clarity, confidence and critical thought, it's magic. And it starts with bringing the goalposts closer.

I also strongly believe that this involves working in increments. This only works once students have mastered each success criteria in isolation. Once they have the opening, then show them precise detail. Only once they have mastered this, move onto the explanation. This way the 'goalposts' are closer – they find one achievable target before moving on to the next in the writing process.

 HACK #4

Model the process, not just the product: Modelling isn't about showing students a perfect paragraph and saying "do that." It's about revealing the messy thinking that gets you there. This is also an opportunity to normalise error and uncertainty, while promoting metacognitive talk in the class room.

In practice

- Use live modelling on the board or visualiser. Draft a paragraph with the class. Narrate your thinking aloud: "I'm choosing this piece of evidence because it directly supports my argument. I'm adding 'this suggests that...' to link back to the question."
- A key strategy that I have used for several years is an "extended margin". This is when, while modelling a paragraph, students have a margin at the side. In this they write either the success criteria or the questions that I would ask myself for each stage of the writing process. Sometimes, they write these questions alongside my model, other times they then use these questions to complete their own paragraph, utilising my thoughts rather than copying my paragraph.
- Invite students to critique your model. "Is my analysis strong enough?" "Could I use more precise vocabulary?" Make some deliberate mistakes or create a model at the level which students in your class are working at, asking them to improve and to guide their answer into the next level. Bounce questions around students to improve vocabulary development and keep the answers concise.
- Leave deliberate mistakes for students to spot – this promotes metacognition (EEF, 2021). Be wary of "the curse of the expert" when you are writing models. Ensure that the model is the quality and length that students would be able and expected to replicate under exam pressures – there's no point showing them something that is unobtainable or too complex – this can switch most students off.
- Later, students try the process independently, with prompts faded over time. When to fade a part of the scaffold is dependent not only on class level, but student level.

The theory

Rosenshine (2012) emphasises the power of worked examples and guided practice. By "thinking aloud," we reduce cognitive load and make expert decision-making visible (Sweller, 1988).

HACK #5

Build writing from talk: Students often say what they can't yet write. Structured oracy helps bridge the gap.

In practice

- Use Think–Pair–Share before essay writing. Ask: "What's the most important cause of the Civil War?" Listen for phrasing and reasoning.
- Capture their verbal responses on the board. Highlight key analytical verbs – "demonstrates", "reveals", "suggests".
- Move from oral rehearsal to written output. "Let's take your sentence and write it exactly as you said it."

When students hear the rhythm of analysis, they can replicate it in writing.

The theory

Mercer (2000) describes talk as "the bridge between speech and thought." By encouraging exploratory talk, we help students internalise disciplinary reasoning before formalising it in text.

Final thought

Teaching writing in history isn't about producing mini academics – it's about giving students the tools to make sense of the past in their own words. Writing is how they synthesise, argue and take ownership of knowledge.

When a student who once said "I hate essays" hands in a piece that opens with, "The Reformation was not inevitable; it was a collision of belief, politics and ambition," you realise it's not just writing practice. It's transformation.

Our job is to make that possible – to bring the goalposts close enough for every student to score, but still left far enough away to make it feel like a victory when they do.

CHAPTER 5:
VOCABULARY DEVELOPMENT
– GIVING STUDENTS
THE LANGUAGE OF HISTORY

In the history classroom, vocabulary isn't an add-on. It's central. Our students are expected to read challenging texts, understand abstract concepts and write extended analytical responses – all while using precise, disciplinary language. If we don't explicitly teach the language of history, we're building our curriculum on sand.

I'll admit, I didn't always see it this way. Early in my teaching career, I'd stumble across students using the word empire interchangeably with country, or referring to monarchs as "presidents from the olden days." They could pronounce revolution, but when asked what it meant, I'd get answers ranging from "a war" to "something that spins."

These weren't lazy students, they were students who didn't have the language to access the discipline. And once you see vocabulary not as decoration but as a key that unlocks understanding, it changes everything.

Quigley (2018) calls vocabulary "a proxy for academic success," and the Education Endowment Foundation (EEF, 2019) lists explicit vocabulary instruction as one of the most impactful strategies for disadvantaged learners. Young (2014) reminds us that "powerful knowledge" is often encoded in words – the technical and conceptual terms that allow us to think beyond our own experiences.

In history, this matters more than almost anywhere else. Our subject is full of loaded, nuanced terms: reformation, appeasement, imperialism, republic, propaganda. Without secure understanding, students are left decoding content they can't fully grasp. Vocabulary is, quite literally, the language of power in our discipline.

So how do we teach it well – not as a quick starter activity, but as an integral thread running through everything we do? Over the years, I've developed a series of practical hacks to build vocabulary fluency, confidence and curiosity in my classroom.

HACK #1

Reading aloud and choral repetition: It starts with sound. Before students can write or apply new vocabulary, they need to hear it and say it correctly. Pronunciation is often overlooked, yet it's the first barrier for many students – especially those with EAL backgrounds or weaker literacy.

In practice
When introducing a new term, I always:

1. Display it clearly on the board.
2. Say it aloud slowly and clearly.
3. Have students repeat it together – choral repetition.
4. Break it into syllables if needed (e.g. "ap-pease-ment").
5. Return to it throughout the lesson whenever it reappears.

For instance, when teaching feudalism, I'll say:

"Let's all try that – feudalism. Again. Good. Now turn to your partner and use it in a sentence: 'Feudalism was the system that structured medieval society.'"

If a student mispronounces it, I don't correct them harshly. I model it again and praise the attempt. We build confidence before precision.

This strategy also works brilliantly for complex or foreign-origin terms – Reichstag, Gulag, bourgeoisie. By repeating them aloud, students start to own them. These choral reading strategies are also effective when reading interpretations or guided reading texts. If you count down and begin reading with the class, students then continue reading as a group. Although this can take some time to embed, it means that students are able to see the vocabulary used within academic texts, and can learn from their peers and those with higher levels of literacy how to say them in practice.

The theory
Explicit rehearsal supports the phonological loop of working memory (Baddeley, 2000). It also reduces affective barriers – students are far more likely to write a word they've confidently spoken.

HACK #2

Define and check for understanding: Once students can say a word, they need to understand it – properly. Too often, I've seen vocabulary lists handed out like spelling sheets, where "define" means "copy the dictionary." But disciplinary language doesn't always translate neatly into dictionary form.

In practice
Take the word "revolution".

- In English, it might mean something turning or spinning.
- In science, it's a planetary orbit.
- In history, it's a fundamental change in society, politics or economy – often sudden or transformative.

I teach this distinction explicitly. On the board, we create a quick comparison table:

Subject	Meaning of "revolution"
English	To revolve or turn
Science	The orbit of one body around another
History	A rapid and significant change in power or structure

Then, we use mini whiteboards to check understanding:

- "Give me one example of a revolution from history."
- "What might make a revolution successful?"

Students write and hold up their answers – low stakes, instant feedback.

You can also use Frayer models (definition, example, non-example, image) or word scrambles to test comprehension.

The theory
Quigley (2018) and Beck *et al.* (2002) highlight the importance of contextualised vocabulary teaching. Students remember words better when they learn them in use, not isolation.

 HACK #3

Build fluency through use: Vocabulary only sticks when it's used repeatedly and meaningfully. I treat every new word as a recurring character in the story of the unit – it reappears in discussion, writing and retrieval.

In practice

When teaching the causes of the French Revolution, I display a mini word bank:

- Aristocracy
- Clergy
- Bourgeoisie
- Taxation
- Liberty

Throughout the lesson, I use cold calling to prompt application:

- "Khalid, can you use 'aristocracy' in a sentence that links to inequality?"
- "Priya, how might 'bourgeoisie' relate to the Enlightenment?"

Later, during written tasks, I include sentence stems:

- "The aristocracy resisted reform because..."
- "The bourgeoisie supported change due to..."

By hearing and writing the same words in varied contexts, students gain confidence and accuracy.

The theory

According to Rosenshine (2012), frequent review and practice are essential for transfer into long-term memory. Each re-use strengthens connections between concept and term.

HACK #4

Plan for retrieval: Vocabulary instruction isn't a one-off – it's a process of spaced retrieval. If we want words to move from working to long-term memory, students must revisit them regularly.

In practice

- Start lessons with Do Now retrieval tasks that mix old and new vocabulary:
    - "Define 'appeasement'."
    - "Which term describes Britain's policy toward Hitler before 1939?"
- Run mini quizzes where students match terms to definitions or correct misuses.
- Include vocabulary flashbacks in homework or revision.

Our department also maintains a Tier 3 vocabulary tracker. For each unit, we log key terms and where they reappear in later topics. For example, "empire", introduced in Year 7, resurfaces in Year 9 when studying decolonisation. This ensures cumulative exposure.

The theory

The spacing effect (Cepeda *et al.*, 2006) and retrieval practice (Karpicke and Roediger, 2008) are proven memory enhancers. Revisiting vocabulary over time ensures durability of learning.

HACK #5

Break vocabulary into tiers: Be deliberate about which words to prioritise. Beck *et al.* (2002) outline three tiers of vocabulary that every teacher should know:

- Tier 1: Everyday language (e.g., king, war, people).
- Tier 2: Cross-disciplinary academic terms (e.g., evaluate, contrast, impact).
- Tier 3: Subject-specific words (e.g., feudalism, appeasement, suffrage).

In practice

When teaching the Suffragette movement, I display a colour-coded list:

- Tier 1: vote
- Tier 2: protest, reform, equality
- Tier 3: suffrage, enfranchisement, militancy

We discuss:

- "Which of these words might appear in other subjects?"
- "Which are unique to history?"

Students then sort mixed words into their correct tiers using cards or digital drag-and-drop tools.

The theory

Explicit tiering helps teachers target cognitive demand appropriately (EEF, 2019). Focusing on Tier 2 and 3 vocabulary improves comprehension and writing precision.

HACK #6

Use vocabulary throughout the learning cycle: Vocabulary shouldn't live at the start of lessons – it should appear before, during and after learning.

In practice

- **Before reading:** Preteach key terms from upcoming texts. If you're studying the Treaty of Versailles, ensure students know "reparations", "mandate" and "territorial loss" first.
- **During reading:** Pause to unpack new words in context. Highlight and annotate them together.
- **During writing:** Provide word banks and challenge boxes. "Try to include at least three of today's key words."
- **During feedback:** Comment not only on knowledge but language. "Could you use a more specific term than 'leader'? Perhaps 'dictator' or 'autocrat'?"

Consistency turns vocabulary from a task into a habit.

The theory

The EEF (2021) stresses that disciplinary literacy requires sustained attention across the learning cycle. Embedding language in each phase deepens understanding.

HACK #7

Get students talking about words: Make vocabulary visible and alive in your classroom culture. When students feel ownership of words, they remember them.

In practice

- **Word of the week:** Display a challenging term with its definition and example and include this in your lesson hypothesis and the crux of lesson objectives. Ask students to highlight the term in their writing, encouraging them to discuss it correctly. Discuss how it might appear across topics.
- **Vocabulary treasure hunts:** Give students a short source and ask them to highlight all Tier 2 and 3 terms.
- **Glossary journals:** Each student maintains their own illustrated glossary – definition, context and a self-written example sentence. Frayer models and dual coding are also big wins to ensure students are using the vocabulary effectively.
- **Oracy activities:** Ask, "Explain 'imperialism' to your partner as if they've never heard the word before."

A personal favourite is a Word Debate. I write two similar terms on the board – propaganda vs persuasion, dictatorship vs autocracy – and ask which is more appropriate for a given historical example. It sparks nuanced discussion about meaning and precision.

The theory

Quigley (2022) highlights that oral rehearsal bridges comprehension and application. Talking about words creates semantic depth, making them easier to recall later.

Final thought

Vocabulary is not separate from knowledge – it is knowledge. It's the thread that connects concepts, the language that lets students think and argue like historians.

When students begin to use "appeasement", "enfranchisement" and "industrialisation" with confidence – when they not only know the words but use them to reason – that's when you see genuine empowerment.

Because teaching history isn't just about what happened. It's about giving students the words to make sense of what happened. And when they find those words, they start to see that history isn't someone else's story – it's theirs too.

CHAPTER 6:
QUESTIONING –
THE ART OF THINKING ALOUD

If there's one constant in every history classroom, it's the hum of questions. They fill the air. "Why did that happen?" "What do you think the source means?" "Who was to blame?" Questioning is our most powerful teaching tool – and sometimes, our most underused one.

Good questioning is far more than checking for understanding. It's how we make students think. It's how we model the historian's mind – curious, sceptical, analytical. It's also how we build classroom culture: a place where students feel safe to get things wrong and brave enough to have a go.

Early in my career, I thought good questioning meant asking lots of questions. The more hands up, the better, right? But I learned quickly that quantity isn't quality. A flurry of "What year was this?" or "Who was the king then?" checks memory, not understanding. Real questioning digs deeper. It unsettles certainty. It gets students to think aloud, to disagree politely, to reconsider what they thought they knew.

Wiliam (2011) says, "Classroom questioning is not a test of memory, it's a rehearsal for thinking." That's the heart of it. In history, our questions can shift students from surface recall to conceptual depth – from "What happened?" to "Why does it matter?" and "How might someone else see this differently?"

Over time, I've learned to treat questioning as both an art and a structure. It needs planning, but it also needs instinct. Below are the hacks I've developed for using questioning to move students from recall to reasoning, from passive learning to active thinking.

HACK #1

Plan the questions, not just the content: We often plan what we'll teach but not what we'll ask. Yet the right question can turn a routine lesson into a moment of insight.

In practice

When planning a lesson, write three key questions in your plan:

- A recall question (e.g., "Who was involved in the Peasants' Revolt?")
- A conceptual question (e.g., "Why do you think the peasants revolted?")
- A disciplinary question (e.g., "How might historians disagree about why the revolt happened?")

By deliberately sequencing them, you take students from factual grounding to analytical thought. Knowing your students well is key to this being successful: which students struggle with recall, which are you pushing with the disciplinary questions? It is essential to plan not only which questions you are asking but who you are going to ask the questions of to ensure that they have the maximum impact.

In a Year 9 lesson on the causes of the World War I, I might start with: "What do we already know about alliances?" Then move to: "How could alliances meant to protect peace actually lead to war?" And finally: "Would a historian writing in 1919 answer that question differently from one writing in 2024?"

Each step adds complexity – scaffolding thinking just as we scaffold writing.

The theory

Rosenshine (2012) notes that effective teachers "ask a large number of questions and check for understanding frequently," but Counsell (2018) reminds us that in history, the type of question matters as much as the frequency.

HACK #2

Cold call with warmth: Cold calling has a reputation for anxiety, but used well creates equity, so questioning stops being a game for the confident few.

In practice

Let students know from the start that anyone can be asked, but that it's never a test – it's an invitation to think.

- Use neutral phrasing: "I'm going to come to you next, just to hear what you're thinking."
- Allow pauses. Silence is golden. Give students "wait time" (Rowe, 1974) before responding.
- Step up from a Think–Pair–Share. Allow students a moment to bullet point down their ideas during this thinking time – this allows me to see that they are using the time effectively (not just thinking about what is for lunch) while also giving the students that lack confidence something to refer back to. In the share part of the task, ask students to add additional ideas in their books from their partner's discussion. When sharing with the class, cold call, but make this open: "tell me one thing you discussed" or "Hannah, what did Ramesh say?" By building in these layers you can then utilise the hands up of those wanting to share more ideas, after checking the understanding of those key students.

When discussing the causes of the English Civil War, I might ask: "Was religion or power more important in starting the war?" Then I'll give thirty seconds of silence.

You can almost hear the thinking.

When I call on a student, if they're unsure, I say: "That's fine – what are you leaning towards?" or "Can anyone build on what they said?" Sometimes, getting them to repeat a correct answer, or reminding students that you will come back to them for the answer later in the lesson means that the opt out students know that there is nowhere to hide. This shifts questioning from fear to exploration.

The theory

Sherrington (2019) argues that effective questioning "balances high accountability with high trust." Cold calling works when students know the classroom is a place of intellectual safety, not embarrassment.

HACK #3

Use question ladders: Good questions come in sequences. Instead of jumping straight to evaluation, build from comprehension to inference to analysis.

In practice

The ladder a source lesson on a World War I recruitment poster might look like this:

1. **Comprehension:** "What can you see in this image?"
2. **Context:** "When and why might this have been created?"

3. **Inference:** "What message is the artist trying to send?"

4. **Evaluation:** "How effective do you think this source would have been at the time?"

Students climb the ladder with you. Over time, they start to internalise it – asking themselves those same questions when they encounter new sources.

The theory

Vygotsky (1978) described learning as movement through the zone of proximal development. Question ladders act as scaffolds, allowing students to reach conceptual levels they couldn't access unaided.

HACK #4

Encourage students to ask questions too: Some of the best thinking in my classroom has come not from my questions, but from those of students. However, this doesn't happen automatically. You have to model it and reward curiosity.

In practice

- After introducing a new topic, ask students to write one question they'd like to answer. For example, after showing images of the Berlin Wall, I ask, "What do you wonder?" Responses range from "Why did they build it?" to "What happened to families separated by it?"
- Return to their questions at the end of the unit and ask them to answer one using evidence.

This transforms enquiry from teacher-led to shared exploration.

The theory

Leat (1998) found that students who generate their own questions show higher engagement and deeper comprehension. Questioning isn't just something we do to students – it's something we should teach them to do for themselves.

HACK #5

Probe, don't pounce: Sometimes a student gives an answer that's half-right, or not quite there. This is where probing questions shine.

In practice

Instead of "No, that's wrong," try:

- "Tell me more about that."
- "What makes you think that?"
- "Can you link that to something else we've studied?"

For example, in a Year 8 lesson on the Reformation:

Student: "Henry wanted to marry Anne Boleyn."

Teacher: "He did. But was that the only reason for the break with Rome?"

Student: "No – there was money and power too."

That small nudge turns a partial answer into a causal explanation.

Plan these questions in advance. Who will you ask which questions? Which students would be better cold called after a Think Pair Share to build confidence? Who needs higher tiered questions to push analytical thinking?

I used to think I 'knew' questioning, but recently taking the moment to plan the questions before the lesson has been a better tool than any number of slides!

The theory

Wiliam (2011) highlights that formative questioning should improve thinking, not simply measure it. Probing questions extend cognition and build self-correction.

HACK #6

Use discussion routines: Structured discussion routines give questioning momentum and inclusivity.

In practice

- **No opt-out:** If a student struggles, support them with scaffolding, then return to them later for another go.
- **Think–Pair–Share:** Give quiet processing time before public response.
- **Pose–Pause–Bounce–Pounce:** Ask, pause, bounce to another student for a build, then return.

Example:

"Why did Britain appease Hitler?" (**Pose**)

[**Pause** for 10 seconds]

"Trinika, what do you think?"

"To avoid war."

"Jamie, can you build on that?" (**Bounce**)

"Because they weren't ready to fight yet."

"Trinika, do you agree with Jamie's reasoning?" (**Pounce** back)

Suddenly, you have dialogue, not ping-pong questioning.

The theory

Lemov (2021) argues that structured dialogue increases participation and accountability. The more voices, the deeper the learning.

 HACK #7

Use big questions to anchor units: Each historical topic deserves a "big question" – one that guides enquiry and unites lessons.

In practice

At the start of a unit, I display the key question in bold on the board and refer to it every lesson. For example:

- "Was the British Empire a force for good?"
- "Did the Industrial Revolution improve people's lives?"
- "How far was the Cold War inevitable?"

Every lesson, I link back: "So, based on today's lesson, how might we start to answer our big question differently?"

By the end, students aren't just learning facts – they're shaping an argument.

The theory

Counsell (2018) calls these "enquiry questions" – a means of framing historical knowledge within purpose and narrative.

Final thought

The best questioning feels like conversation, not interrogation. It creates an atmosphere where curiosity thrives and wrong answers become routes to understanding.

If there's one sound that tells me a lesson is going well, it's that collective hum of thinking – the quiet pause before an idea lands, the murmur of students debating meaning. That's the sound of history being learned, not as a script, but as an ongoing dialogue.

CHAPTER 7:
CURRICULUM COHERENCE
AND DESIGN – CRAFTING
A HISTORICAL JOURNEY

Every few years, someone in the department says, "We really should look at the curriculum." Everyone nods, then glances at the marking pile. Curriculum work always feels important but never urgent – until you realise the gaps are showing.

A history curriculum isn't a checklist of content. It's the story we choose to tell about the past and the route we take through it. Coherence is what stops that story from feeling like a box set watched out of order. Students shouldn't be surprised when the causes of World War I make more sense because of what they learned about empire in Year 8. That's coherence in action.

When I first took on curriculum planning, I focused on coverage: could we squeeze every period from the Romans to the Cold War into three years? The result looked busy but felt bitty. Students remembered fragments, not frameworks. So we started again – less "What do we have to cover?" and more "What do we want them to understand about how history works?"

HACK #1

Work backwards from the big ideas: Begin with the disciplinary end-points. What do you want your historians to be able to do by the end of key stage 3? Explain change? Evaluate interpretations? Build arguments?

Once you've nailed the outcomes, build backwards. Each unit should rehearse a part of that skill. For example, if you want Year 9 students to write about causation confidently, plant the language of causation early in Year 7. Link it explicitly when you revisit it later.

In practice

When we redesigned our sequence, we stuck giant paper strips along the corridor wall and plotted units in order. Then we asked, "What thread runs through this?" If we couldn't find one, we rewrote the enquiry. It felt messy, but it made the curriculum ours – a shared narrative rather than a hand-me-down scheme.

HACK #2

Thread, don't stack: Chronology matters, but sequence isn't the same as coherence. It's easy to pile topics one on top of another and call it progression. Instead, identify a few recurring concepts – power, belief, conflict, migration – and keep looping back to them.

In practice

At the start of each unit, we remind students: "You've met this idea before." When studying the Peasants' Revolt, we ask, "How did people challenge power here?" Later, during the Industrial Revolution, "How are these protests similar or different?" By GCSE, students can track "power and protest" across centuries without prompting.

One simple change made this visible: every student has a "concept tracker" at the front of their book. They highlight where each concept appears. It sounds small, but it's become our golden thread – literally.

HACK #3

Build diversity in, not on: A coherent curriculum represents the diversity of the past throughout, not as an appendix. When we reviewed our scheme, we realised the global dimension mostly appeared in stand-alone lessons on the empire or slavery. We wanted integration, not tokenism.

Now, global links appear everywhere. In a lesson on the Industrial Revolution, we follow a bale of cotton from India to Manchester. When teaching World War I, we include soldiers from across the empire. Students start to see that British history has always been connected history.

A Year 8 pupil once said, "It's like we're zooming out and seeing the whole world map." That's exactly the coherence we were aiming for.

HACK #4

Depth beats breadth (if it's chosen wisely): We all want to "get to" the 20th century, but racing through the past doesn't build understanding. Choose depth where it earns its keep. A well-selected deep dive can illuminate wider patterns far better than a whistle-stop tour.

In practice

We now pair every long enquiry with a short comparative "snapshot". Studying the English Civil War? Spend one lesson on the Fronde in France. Exploring industrialisation? Glimpse what's happening in Japan. It keeps the global picture alive without derailing the main narrative.

HACK #5

Show the map: Students can't follow a journey they can't see. At the start of each year, we give them a one-page "curriculum map" showing when and why each topic appears. In lessons, we refer back to it constantly – "Remember where we are on the map."

That small visual reminder helps them anchor new knowledge. Retrieval quizzes draw on earlier units, reinforcing the sense of journey: "What did we learn in Year 7 that helps us here?" The answer is usually more than they expect.

HACK #6

Keep it alive: A coherent curriculum isn't finished, it's maintained. After each assessment, we ask if students made the connections we expected. If not, we tweak the sequence. Sometimes that means moving a unit, sometimes rewriting an enquiry question.

Coherence grows through conversation. The best curriculum meetings aren't about admin – they're about ideas. They start with "Why are we teaching this?" and end with "How can we make it clearer next time?"

Final thought

Curriculum coherence is slow-burn work. You won't feel the impact overnight, but when you hear a Year 9 student link the Black Death to changes in land ownership or connect the Reformation to today's debates about belief, you know the threads are holding.

That's the reward: students who see history not as fragments, but as a story they understand – and can tell for themselves.

CHAPTER 8:
DISCIPLINARY THINKING
AND HISTORICAL ENQUIRY –
HELPING STUDENTS THINK
LIKE HISTORIANS

Every history teacher knows that moment – you ask a question about causes or consequences, and a hand shoots up confidently: "It happened because Henry VIII wanted a son."

Factually true. But when you probe further – "Was that the only reason?" – silence. It's not that students don't know – they're just not yet thinking historically. They see history as a collection of stories rather than a discipline with its own habits of mind.

Disciplinary thinking is what turns history from memory work into meaning-making. It's about getting students to do history, not merely learn about it – to question, interpret and argue using evidence. Counsell (2018) calls this "seeing the curriculum as the progression model." Each time students revisit a historical concept – causation, change, significance – they're not simply revising; they're refining the intellectual tools that make them historians.

When I started teaching, I thought enquiry questions were just hooks – a bit of mystery to make a lesson fun. But true historical enquiry isn't window dressing, it's the engine that drives disciplinary understanding. It invites students to inhabit the historian's mindset, asking not only what happened, but how we know and why it matters.

HACK #1

Structure learning around powerful enquiry questions: A strong enquiry question gives coherence, direction and purpose to a sequence of lessons. It acts like a thread through the tapestry.

In practice

Instead of planning a unit called The Tudors, start with a question that demands argument and evidence:

- "Was Henry VIII a hero or a tyrant?"
- "Did Elizabeth I rule more with luck or skill?"
- "How revolutionary was the Reformation?"

At the beginning of the unit, I ask students for a hunch – a first response. Midway through, we revisit it. By the end, they write a final answer supported by evidence. Watching their reasoning evolve is powerful; you can literally see disciplinary thinking develop on the page.

To model this, I make my own reasoning visible: "If I argue he was a tyrant, what evidence supports that? What counter-examples challenge it?" That constant weighing-up – as Wineburg (2001) notes – is the hallmark of expert historical reasoning.

The theory

Ashby and Lee (2000) describe historical enquiry as progression from collecting information to constructing arguments. A good question anchors that progression and gives knowledge purpose.

HACK #2

Teach second-order concepts explicitly: Students need to grasp that history is built on conceptual **lenses**: cause, consequence, change, continuity, similarity, difference, significance, and interpretation.

In practice

Create concept cards or wall displays defining each lens with examples:

Concept	Guiding question
Cause	Why did it happen?
Change	How did things develop over time?
Significance	Why does it matter?

When studying the Industrial Revolution, I'll ask:

- "If we use the concept of change, what do we see?"
- "If we switch to significance, what shifts in our interpretation?"

By toggling between lenses, students realise history isn't one story but a series of perspectives shaped by the questions we ask.

The theory

Seixas (2006) identifies these as "historical thinking concepts." When taught deliberately, they move students beyond narrative recall into analytical reasoning.

HACK #3

Model the historian's process: Historical thinking is visible thinking. Students must see how historians approach a problem, not just the polished conclusion.

In practice

When introducing a new source, narrate your thought process aloud: "First, I check who wrote it – that tells me perspective. Next, the date – was it before or after the event? That affects reliability."

Then ask students to think aloud as you have done, in pairs, mirroring the process. Over time this metacognitive routine becomes habit.

Extend it into writing: draft a paragraph live under the visualiser, verbalising choices as you go. "I'm linking this cause to show priority...I'll add 'however' to show contrast." Students begin to hear the historian's internal monologue and eventually develop one of their own.

The theory

Rosenshine (2012) calls this cognitive apprenticeship: making expert thinking explicit so novices can imitate and internalise it.

 HACK #4

Embed enquiry across key stages: Enquiry shouldn't stop at key stage 3. It should spiral upwards into GCSE and A-level, with increasing complexity and independence.

In practice

- **KS3:** Enquiry might culminate in a short analytical paragraph.
- **KS4:** It becomes a structured essay comparing factors.
- **KS5:** Students evaluate interpretations using historiography.

For instance, in Year 8 we ask: "Why did Parliament win the Civil War?" By Year 13, that matures into: "Was Charles I's downfall inevitable?"

The continuity of concept builds disciplinary maturity. Students see that the same thinking structures underpin every phase of study.

The theory

Bruner's (1960) spiral curriculum and Willingham's (2009) research on schema building both stress that complexity should deepen through repetition and refinement.

HACK #5

Let students see historians at work: Expose learners to real historical debate; it shows that disagreement is the discipline.

In practice

- Use short extracts from contrasting historians – Elton vs Starkey on Henry VIII, or Ferguson vs Marxist readings of empire.
- Run a "Historian of the Week" spotlight with a short summary of their argument and a short student response: "Do you agree? Why?"
- Ask: "Why might their background or context shape their view?"

When students realise historians disagree – and that evidence allows multiple readings – they start to read with both scepticism and empathy. It shifts them from absorbing to interrogating.

The theory

Wineburg (2001) calls this sourcing and corroboration – evaluating who says what and why, not simply memorising facts.

HACK #6

Use retrieval to connect enquiries: Coherence across enquiries is built through retrieval and reflection.

In practice

Start each new topic with bridging questions:

- "What similarities can you spot between medieval rebellion and modern protest?"
- "How has the idea of power changed since we studied the Tudors?"

Have students create cumulative concept maps that expand term by term – visual webs of how key ideas reappear. When a Year 9 student remarks, "This is like the empire we studied last year," you know disciplinary thinking is taking root.

The theory

Retrieval builds schema. By spacing and interleaving concepts, we move understanding from short-term recall to long-term disciplinary awareness.

Final thought

Disciplinary thinking is what turns history from story-time into scholarship. It's the moment students stop parroting "because Henry wanted a son" and start asking, "Why do historians disagree about whether that mattered most?"

Teaching history isn't just about giving students knowledge of the past, it's about giving them the intellectual habits to question it. When they start arguing like historians – using evidence, weighing interpretations, revisiting ideas – you know they've moved from learning history to doing it.

CHAPTER 9: INTERPRETATIONS – SEEING THE PAST THROUGH MANY EYES

If you ever want proof that history isn't fixed, ask two students who started the same topic to summarise it six weeks later.

One will say, "The Empire made Britain rich." The other will say, "The Empire exploited people."

Both are right – and both are incomplete. That's the joy and the challenge of teaching interpretations.

Interpretations work throws students into the deep end of historical thinking. It's not enough to know what happened – they have to grapple with how people have understood what happened, and why those understandings shift over time.

When I first started teaching, I dreaded interpretations. They felt abstract, detached from the thrilling stories that made me love history. Over time I realised this is the disciplinary heartbeat of our subject. It's where students learn that history is not the past itself – it's the ongoing conversation about the past. Once that clicks, everything else in the curriculum starts to make sense.

As an examiner, this is a key skill where I see students become blinded by provenance. They are quick to throw the word 'bias' around – in my classroom this word is banned. A focus on bias can lead to students immediately branding an interpretation as 'untrustworthy' but even a speech by Hitler helps to shape understanding of Nazi goals – this surface-level analysis must be deepened.

HACK #1

Demystify what an interpretation is: Students often confuse interpretations with sources: "But Miss, this is written after the event – isn't that just a secondary source?"

We need to make the distinction clear. I use the metaphor of a painting:

- The source is the brushstroke – direct evidence from the time.
- The interpretation is the finished portrait – someone's attempt to show what they think the past looked like.

In practice

We collect examples: textbook extracts, historians' quotes, documentaries, podcasts, museum plaques, even TikTok explainers. Students see that interpretations come in many forms and that each reflects its creator's context and purpose. We annotate one together, underlining loaded language or selective emphasis. "Why that adjective?" "What might the author want us to think?" The conversation quickly shifts from "What happened?" to "Why tell it this way?"

To reinforce, I'll give them a jumble of statements from historians and journalists about the same event – the fall of the Berlin Wall works well – and ask them to order them from "most celebratory" to "most critical". The debate that follows is pure disciplinary thinking.

The theory

Ashby and Lee (2000) argue that understanding interpretations marks a major cognitive leap: students realise history is constructed, not given.

HACK #2

Make the purpose visible: Every interpretation exists for a reason. Helping students uncover that reason is key.

In practice

When studying the legacy of the British Empire, I present two textbook extracts: one from 1950, one from 2020.

We annotate together: "Who wrote it?" "When?" "What message are they trying to send?" "Who is the audience?"

Then I ask, "How might the timing of each book shape what it says?" Students immediately see that post-war pride and post-colonial critique produce very different stories.

Next, we link it to purpose in our own lives. "If you posted about this on social media, what would you want your followers to think or feel?" That moment of recognition – that all communication has motive – makes the idea stick.

The theory
Wineburg (2001) calls this contextualisation. Historical thinking demands aware-ness of the interpreter's context as much as the event's.

HACK #3

Compare and critique: Comparing interpretations side by side encourages evaluation rather than acceptance.

In practice
For a GCSE unit on the Cold War, we examine how Western and Soviet textbooks describe the Cuban Missile Crisis. Students identify differences in language – "aggressive" vs "defensive." They note what's included, what's omitted, and which voices are missing entirely.

We then write a collective paragraph starting, "Historians might disagree be-cause..." Each group offers a reason grounded in context – political bias, source access, or national pride.

It's brilliant to watch how quickly they stop seeing "difference" as a problem and start seeing it as evidence. The room fills with comments like, "That's interesting – they both use 'freedom' but mean opposite things."

The theory
Seixas and Morton (2013) call this historical perspective-taking, a cornerstone of disciplinary literacy.

HACK #4

Use visual and material interpretations: Interpretations aren't always written: they're painted, sculpted, filmed, staged, tweeted. Visual and material culture opens the door for every learner.

In practice
I show students two depictions of Cromwell – a heroic Victorian portrait and a modern critical one. We ask:

- "What is the artist celebrating or criticising?"
- "What emotions are they trying to provoke?"
- "What might this tell us about their own time?"

The same approach works with film clips, memorials and even coins. I once used the *Horrible Histories* take on the French Revolution alongside a BBC documentary. The laughter turned into analysis within minutes: "This one's trying to entertain. That one's trying to educate."

Later, we visit the local museum. Each student photographs an artefact label and writes a short reflection: "What interpretation is this display promoting?" Those reflections now form part of our departmental display board, showing that interpretation lives beyond the classroom.

The theory
Chapman (2011) stresses that visual and popular interpretations show students how history is continually rewritten for new audiences.

HACK #5

Connect interpretations to assessment: Students often panic at "How useful is this interpretation?" questions. We can demystify them by embedding evaluation language early.

In practice
I use the mnemonic CAMP:

- **Content:** What does it say?
- **Audience:** Who is it for?
- **Motive:** Why was it created?
- **Perspective:** What viewpoint does it show?

We practise CAMP constantly – on political cartoons, film trailers, even teachers' explanations. "What's Miss Chadwick's motive here?" (Cue laughter – and insight.)

By GCSE, students are fluent: "This interpretation is useful because it shows postwar optimism, but limited because it ignores decolonisation." The trick is familiarity – they've analysed so many interpretations informally that the formal question feels natural.

The theory
The EEF (2021) notes that structured frameworks reduce cognitive load. Mnemonics like CAMP free up working memory so that students can focus on argument.

HACK #6

Let students create their own interpretations: Nothing deepens understanding like making one yourself.

In practice
After studying the Black Death, I ask students to produce a modern museum label titled "The Most Significant Impact of the Plague". They must select evidence and justify their interpretation. Others script a short documentary voice-over or write a historian's blog post from a chosen perspective.

In one Year 8 lesson, a student narrated a podcast called "The Peasants' Revolt – A Teenager's Guide". It was witty, accurate and showed complete ownership of the interpretative process. That's what disciplinary confidence looks like.

We finish by displaying their work with labels such as "A 21st-Century Interpretation". It drives home that everything we produce about the past – including this classroom display – is an interpretation.

The theory
Constructivist approaches (Bruner 1960; Vygotsky 1978) highlight that learners build understanding through creation and articulation, not passive absorption.

HACK #7

Link interpretations across time: To make interpretations meaningful, students must see them change.

In practice
We track shifting views of empire, monarchy or suffrage across centuries. On the board I draw a timeline labelled "Changing Views of the British Empire". At intervals we pin short extracts: Victorian pride, 1950s nostalgia, 1980s revisionism, 2020s reflection. Students annotate why tone changes: "New evidence", "Cultural attitudes", "Modern values".

This longitudinal view helps them see that reinterpretation is inevitable. Each generation writes the past it needs.

The theory

Collins (2018) describes this as the historiography of the classroom – teaching students to see history as evolving scholarship rather than static truth.

Final thought

Teaching interpretations isn't about making students cynical. It's about making them critical. It's the antidote to "single-story" history. When students realise every account carries perspective, they start reading the world differently.

In the end, that's the most powerful thing we can teach: that understanding history isn't about finding the answer, but learning how to ask better questions – and how to listen to the many answers that come back.

CHAPTER 10:
HEARING ALL VOICES –
DIVERSITY AND
REPRESENTATION IN THE
HISTORY CLASSROOM

If you've been teaching for more than five minutes, you'll know that one of the most common questions we ask ourselves is: "Whose story am I telling?"

History, by its nature, has always been selective. We choose, we condense, we frame. Every curriculum is a set of decisions – about what to include, what to leave out and how to link it all together. But as our classrooms grow more diverse in background, experience and voice, the need to tell a wider story becomes both moral and intellectual.

When I first started teaching, I didn't think much about diversity in my curriculum. I was too busy trying to keep on top of the lessons, the marking, the logistics. But when the Colston statue came down and global conversations about race, identity and representation entered our classrooms, I found myself reflecting deeply. How well does my curriculum reflect the world my students live in?

That reflection wasn't just about adding "new" stories. It was about recognising that broadening perspectives makes everyone a better historian. Diversity isn't a favour to some students - it strengthens the disciplinary heart of our subject. It teaches empathy, complexity and humility. It helps students see that history isn't owned by one voice, one country or one kind of person.

Counsell (2020) puts it like this: "A diverse curriculum isn't an optional extra; it's the foundation of good curriculum thinking." Diversity and coherence aren't in opposition - they belong together. A curriculum that genuinely hears all voices allows students to see history as a web, not a straight line.

HACK #1

Start with representation - let students see themselves: Representation is not a buzzword - it's a bridge. When students see themselves in the curriculum, the subject becomes alive and personal. It moves from their history teacher's passion to their history.

In practice
Start small. Audit your current schemes of work. Ask:

- Whose stories dominate?
- Which voices are missing?
- Where can I include new perspectives without breaking coherence?

For example:

- In teaching the Industrial Revolution, show that Britain's industrial wealth relied on global networks of labour and trade - Indian cotton, Caribbean sugar, African enslavement.
- During World War I, explore how colonial soldiers fought under British command. A single photograph of Sikh or Senegalese troops can open deep conversations about loyalty, identity and empire.
- In Tudor lessons, include John Blanke, the Black trumpeter at Henry VIII's court, and the North African diplomats who visited Elizabeth I.

I often begin these lessons with a simple question: "Who gets remembered, and why?" It's amazing how quickly students grasp that remembering itself is political.

Then, link representation to aspiration. In one Year 9 class, a student quietly said, "Miss, I didn't know people like my grandad were in the war." That moment changed the way the whole class saw the topic - not as distant history, but as family history.

The theory
Bishop (1990) described the curriculum as a space for "mirrors, windows, and sliding doors." Students need to see themselves (mirrors), see others (win-

53

dows), and step into new worlds (doors). When they can do all three, history becomes human.

HACK #2

Don't bolt diversity on – weave it in: There's a danger in treating inclusivity as something to "fit in" rather than something to build from. When we confine diverse histories to Black History Month or one "global" lesson at the end of term, we unintentionally signal that these voices are additional, not essential.

In practice
When reviewing a scheme, I use a quick test: "If I removed this 'diversity' lesson, would students' understanding of the topic change?"

If the answer is no, it's tokenism. If the answer is yes – if removing it makes the story incomplete – then it's coherence through inclusion.

For example:

- In our British Empire unit, the Indian Rebellion of 1857 isn't an optional case study – it's central to understanding imperial tension and resistance.
- In Elizabethan England, we teach the transatlantic world not as background context but as a live part of England's economy and moral dilemma.
- When teaching Civil Rights, we go global – South Africa, the Caribbean, India – showing that the language of protest transcends borders.

One small but powerful change was rewriting enquiry questions to include agency. Instead of "How did the Empire affect the colonies?" we ask, "How did people across the Empire resist and reshape British rule?" The shift in wording reframes the story without losing coherence.

The theory
Cooper (2017) warns that "diversity without structure is tokenism; coherence without diversity is exclusion." The goal is both: a curriculum that is intellectually rigorous and globally aware.

HACK #3

Use sources to hear hidden voices: Primary sources are our best allies in rebalancing the narrative. They let students hear the past directly – unfiltered, human and often surprising.

In practice

I often begin with paired or contrasting voices:

- When studying slavery, students analyse extracts from Olaudah Equiano's autobiography alongside plantation records.
- In World War I, we read letters from colonial soldiers describing both pride and disillusionment.
- During the Suffragette movement, we compare Emmeline Pankhurst's speeches with those of working-class campaigners like Annie Kenney.

We ask simple but powerful questions:

- "What changes when we switch whose voice we listen to?"
- "What do we lose if this source isn't heard?"

Sometimes the answers are profound. A Year 8 student once said, "We keep talking about people being given rights, but they fought for them." That insight came from hearing voices that textbooks often skip.

The theory

Wineburg (2001) calls this the "unnatural act" of sourcing – questioning not just what is said, but who says it and why. Listening to hidden voices teaches scepticism and empathy, the twin pillars of historical literacy.

HACK #4

Connect the global and the local: Students understand global issues best when they see how those issues played out locally. It's what makes history feel real.

In practice

When teaching migration, I ask students to explore our town's census records, mapping how names and places of birth change over time. We link these to national stories – Windrush, Commonwealth migration, EU expansion.

We also invite families and local community members to share lived histories. One student's grandfather spoke about arriving from Jamaica in the 1960s. For that student, history stopped being abstract – it became heritage.

When teaching the Cold War, we look at how global tension affected local lives – from peace marches to nearby nuclear bunkers. It sparks curiosity: "What did this mean for our community?"

Students often say this is when history feels most "alive." They see that world history is also their history.

The theory

Vygotsky's (1978) socio-cultural theory reminds us that meaning grows through context and connection. Linking global to local turns curriculum knowledge into lived understanding.

 HACK #5

Create space for student-led enquiry: Nothing transforms ownership like asking students to research their own histories. When they become knowledge-creators, the power dynamic of the classroom shifts.

In practice

Our department runs a project called "Histories Hidden in Plain Sight". Students choose a forgotten figure or event and create a short presentation, article or digital exhibit. Past topics include:

- Noor Inayat Khan and the SOE
- Caribbean nurses in the NHS
- The Amritsar Massacre
- The 1981 Brixton Riots

We showcase their work in a History Fair evening and invite families to attend. Every year, I'm amazed by the depth of research. One group traced a relative who had served in the British Indian Army during World War I. Another created a mini documentary on Asian suffragettes.

The energy in the room that evening says it all: history isn't something done to them – it's something they can shape.

The theory

Dewey (1938) argued that inquiry is at the heart of democratic education. When students lead enquiry, they learn that history is not inherited – it's investigated.

 HACK #6

Challenge canonical narratives: Hearing all voices also means interrogating how "official" histories are made and maintained.

In practice

I use textbook extracts from different decades and ask: "What's changed? What stayed the same? Why?"

In teaching empire, I show a 1950s textbook describing "the benefits of civilisation" alongside a modern extract highlighting exploitation. Students instantly spot the shift in tone, and we discuss why those shifts occur – new evidence, new values, new audiences.

We extend this to memorials, museum exhibits and films. Who decides how the past is presented? Who gets a statue, a plaque, a film – and who doesn't?

We once held a "museum remix" lesson: students redesigned a local exhibition to include missing voices. The results were creative, challenging and often moving. It was a vivid reminder that history is an ongoing act of interpretation.

The theory

Seixas and Morton (2013) emphasise that disciplinary thinking requires historical perspective-taking: recognising that all histories are constructed through the lenses of context, purpose and power.

HACK #7

Keep the conversation going: A diverse curriculum is never finished. It's not a checklist – it's a living conversation between teachers, students, and society.

In practice

We revisit our schemes of work every summer. We ask:

- "Which units resonated most with students?"
- "Where did we fall back on the same old narratives?"
- "What new scholarship or resources could deepen our approach next year?"

Sometimes the biggest breakthroughs come from small tweaks – a new source, a reframed enquiry question or an unexpected student suggestion. One Year 10 student once asked, "Could we look at how my country was affected by the Cold War?" That single question led to a new micro-study in our scheme – and better global understanding for the whole class.

The theory

Curriculum design is iterative. Counsell (2021) reminds us that coherence isn't about perfection; it's about deliberate, thoughtful evolution.

Final thought

Broadening perspectives isn't about rewriting history – it's about completing it. It's about making the subject richer, deeper, and more truthful.

When students leave our classrooms understanding that there were many voices, many experiences and many truths, they're not just learning about the past – they're learning how to live in the present.

And perhaps that's the ultimate purpose of history: to make us more empathetic, more curious and more connected.

CHAPTER 11: TEACHING A-LEVEL – STRETCHING THE HISTORIANS OF TOMORROW

There's something wonderfully different about an A-level history classroom. The discussions are livelier, the debates fiercer, the essays longer (and occasionally more dramatic). Teaching at this level feels like stepping into the discipline's living heart. But with that excitement comes a certain pressure – not just to cover content, but to cultivate young historians who can think, argue and write with sophistication.

I'll admit: my first year teaching A-level was a shock. I'd just mastered my GCSE pacing when I found myself knee-deep in Russian revolutions, cold coffee and coursework drafts that stretched to small novels. But over time, I've learned that A-level success comes from structure and mindset – from turning uncertainty into intellectual curiosity.

The following hacks are about building that bridge: between guided school learning and genuine scholarly independence.

 HACK #1

Help students understand the leap: The transition from GCSE to A-level is enormous. Students move from clear mark schemes and scaffolded paragraphs to open-ended essays requiring argument, synthesis and judgement.

In practice

In the first week, I show students two responses to the same question – one GCSE-style, one A-level. We annotate them together. They quickly spot what's different:

- Sustained argument
- Integration of historiography
- Thematic structure
- Subtlety of language

We build a "What Makes A-level History?" wall together, adding examples as we go through the year. By demystifying the challenge, you make it conquerable.

The theory

Bruner's (1960) idea of the "spiral curriculum" is key here – each level of education builds on the last, revisiting key ideas with increasing complexity.

HACK #2

Build the knowledge base first: Many students want to debate interpretations before they've learned the story. But as Counsell (2018) rightly reminds us, "there is no argument without knowledge."

In practice

When introducing new units – for example, Russia 1917–1953 – we start with factual fluency: timelines, key terms, sequencing games, short retrieval tasks. Only once students can confidently narrate events do we tackle interpretation debates: "Was Stalin's rise inevitable?" "How do historians explain the Terror?"

We also use "Story So Far" maps at the end of each week – quick visual overviews connecting themes across time. Students refer to these constantly in essays.

The theory

Cognitive load theory (Sweller, 1988) shows that deep reasoning depends on automatic recall of prior knowledge. By securing that base, you free students' working memory for analysis.

 HACK #3

Model the historian's craft: Students need to see what good historical writing looks like – not just read about it.

In practice

Use a visualiser to model paragraph construction live. Narrate your choices: "I'm going to start with an argument, not a fact. Here's my judgement in the first line. Now I'll bring in evidence and counter-evidence."

Then ask students to annotate your model for structure, tone and flow. I also share extracts from real historians' work (Kershaw, MacCulloch, Evans) so students can see how argument sounds in the wild.

The theory

Rosenshine (2012) calls this "explicit modelling." Chiles (2023) reminds us that modelling should show process, not just perfection – demonstrating redrafting, uncertainty and reflection helps students see writing as iterative.

 HACK #4

Make historiography engaging: The word "historiography" terrifies students. It sounds dense, inaccessible, almost elitist. But really, it's just the story of how historians argue – and students love a good argument.

In practice

I tell students that historiography is "history gossip." Who disagreed with whom, and why?

We make debate maps:

- Intentionalists vs Structuralists on Hitler's power.
- Optimists vs Pessimists on Weimar Germany.
- Cold War Orthodox vs Revisionist vs Post-Revisionist interpretations.

Students role-play historians in "conference debates". One takes A.J.P. Taylor, another Kershaw, another Evans – and they debate with evidence. Laughter and learning intertwine beautifully.

The theory

Seixas and Morton (2013) emphasise that understanding interpretation as evolving dialogue deepens disciplinary understanding. It's not about memorising names, it's about recognising how history changes with each new question.

HACK #5

Scaffold coursework and research skills: Independent coursework (NEA) is often where students either thrive or flounder. It's their first taste of real research – but without guidance, it can be overwhelming.

In practice

Break the process into stages:

1. **Proposal and rationale:** Students pitch ideas with research questions.

2. **Annotated bibliography:** Practise summarising and critiquing sources.

3. **Draft structure:** Plan argument before writing.

4. **Checkpoint feedback:** Short, verbal coaching rather than written essays.

We hold a Mini History Conference mid-year where students share progress and get peer feedback. It builds accountability and confidence.

The theory

Bandura's (1997) concept of self-efficacy is central: scaffolding increases competence, which builds confidence, which sustains motivation.

HACK #6

Use feedback as a conversation: A-level marking can consume your life if you let it. The goal isn't to write essays on essays – it's to create feedback that leads to action.

In practice

I use feedback clinics. After returning essays, I project anonymised excerpts and we discuss: "What works here? What could make this stronger?" Then students re-draft in class using colour-coded pens. This makes feedback a live dialogue rather than a static event.

We also use success criteria checklists co-created by students: they assess themselves before submission. It builds ownership and reflection.

The theory

Hattie and Timperley (2007) stress that feedback should answer three questions: "Where am I going?", "How am I going?" and "Where to next?". Chiles (2023) adds that the best feedback focuses on thinking, not just performance.

 **HACK #7**

Keep the love of the subject alive: In all the essay marking and exam anxiety, it's easy to lose the joy that drew us – and our students – to history in the first place. But curiosity is the best stretch.

In practice

We end each half term with a Beyond the Spec lesson – documentaries, podcasts or museum case studies that connect the unit to broader themes. Students choose something that fascinated them and present a short "Historian's Minute" to the class.

I also host history coffee clubs – informal lunchtime meetups where we discuss new films or articles. It sounds small, but it transforms atmosphere.

One Year 13 student once said, "I like that you still love history, Miss. It makes me want to as well." That's the quiet magic of enthusiasm – it's contagious.

The theory

Deci and Ryan's (2000) self-determination theory underlines the importance of autonomy, mastery and purpose for intrinsic motivation. Students who feel ownership of learning stay engaged long after the exams.

Final thought

A-level isn't just another exam stage. It's a turning point, where students discover that history isn't about knowing everything – it's about asking better questions, balancing evidence and embracing complexity.

Our role is to model that intellectual courage – to show that uncertainty isn't weakness, it's inquiry. And when you watch a student construct their first original argument, disagree with a historian respectfully and defend it with evidence – that's when you see them becoming the historians of tomorrow.

CHAPTER 12:
SCAFFOLDING FOR
SUCCESS – SUPPORTING
EVERY LEARNER

This chapter is rooted in a talk I delivered at ResearchEd Warrington in 2025, alongside my brilliant colleague, Holly Crick. We titled it "Scaffolding for Success," and it came from a very real place: our shared experience of watching students become overwhelmed in the history classroom. Not because they weren't capable, but because the support they needed to get there wasn't always clearly built in. It was our attempt to share what we'd learned, what we were still figuring out and what we believed could make the difference.

Scaffolding has always been central to effective teaching, but in the history classroom – where students must wrestle with abstract concepts, diverse content, and high cognitive demand – its importance becomes even more pronounced. Unlike subjects that can follow a more linear structure, history demands layered knowledge and the ability to recall and apply ideas across wide spans of time. This chapter explores how scaffolding can be embedded across the learning cycle, drawing on pedagogical theory, cognitive science and the practical strategies we've trialled and refined in our own classrooms.

We were particularly inspired by the work of Barak Rosenshine, and Tom Sherrington's clear translation (2019) of Rosenshine's Principles of Instruction (2012).

Their emphasis on modelling, guided practice, checking for understanding and gradually fading support helped us to reframe our own approach – not just to planning, but to how we responded in real time to what students did and didn't know. The idea isn't to do the thinking for students – but to show them how to think like historians.

Learning happens when students think hard (Coe *et al.*, 2014), but "thinking hard" doesn't mean being left to flounder. Scaffolding bridges the gap between where students are now and where we want them to be. It's how we make high challenge achievable – without lowering our expectations.

It also reflects what we know from Vygotsky's (1978) concept of the Zone of Proximal Development: students need just enough support to succeed, and just enough challenge to grow. Too much of one, not enough of the other, and progress stalls.

Scaffolding matters not because it simplifies learning, but because it structures it. Structured thinking enables historical thinking. It allows students to build up the skills to tackle interpretations, source analysis, causation and significance, all while managing the complex knowledge required.

HACK #1

Plan from the top, scaffold down: In our early years of teaching, we both made the same mistake – planning for the middle. We'd pitch tasks to where we thought most students were and hope to catch everyone else. But what we learned – and now advocate for – is planning from the top. Design for the highest attainers and then build scaffolded routes for others.

This isn't about adding bolt-on support at the end. It's about designing access from the outset.

- Start with your big historical question and identify the core knowledge students need.
- Break that knowledge into "golden threads" that can be built across the curriculum.
- Plan backward from the end-of-unit tasks so that each lesson builds towards the complexity required.

When we do this well, all students are challenged – and none are excluded. This approach also avoids the trap of over-simplification, which can lead to low engagement and limited progress.

HACK #2

Catch them winning: We introduced this phrase in our talk at ResearchEd, and it really stuck. The idea is simple: make sure every student experiences success early in the lesson. This might mean:

- A Do Now rooted in retrieval from last lesson or last term.
- A hinge question that gives them a quick win.
- A structured pair discussion that builds toward an independent contribution.

We know from cognitive science that success is motivating. It builds momentum. And when students feel like they're winning, they're more willing to take risks later on.

Equally, these early wins can build the kind of classroom culture we all strive for – where students feel secure enough to try, fail and improve. It builds trust.

HACK #3

Use hinge questions to check for understanding: Rosenshine is clear – checking for understanding is non-negotiable. But how we do that matters. We've found hinge questions to be the most efficient, high-leverage way to assess and adapt.

- Build in multiple-choice questions with distractors that reveal misconceptions.
- Plan when these questions will come in your lesson sequence.
- Use whole-class response systems (whiteboards, hands-up, cold call) to gather responses.

And then adjust. Don't plough ahead if half the class didn't get it. Reteach. Re-frame. Regroup. Those that have the understanding could move onto an additional task, or an application of the understanding while working with a small group. These are best used when they check for the understanding of the whole class. This can be through mini whiteboards or the "show me" app – even just writing the letter into their exercise book and asking them to hold it up! This quick check is a way of assessing where to go next within the lesson.

Include some misconceptions in there, push your high prior attainers to explain why it's **not** a particular answer, or why the rest of the class might have fallen into a particular trap you've set.

Hinge questions don't just serve the teacher. They help students check their own understanding too. That metacognitive loop is key to long-term retention.

HACK #4

Scaffold the writing process: Writing in history is hard. It demands structure, fluency and deep content knowledge. We wanted to help students move beyond formulaic paragraphs and actually construct arguments.

So we co-developed a simple, adaptable success criteria structure which was mentioned in chapter 4:

- **Success Criteria 1:** Dynamic Opening Sentence (DOS) – a direct answer to the question.
- **Success Criteria 1:** Evidence– Statistics, People, Events, Dates (SPED).
- **Success Criteria 1:** Explanation – what the evidence shows and why it matters.
- **Success Criteria 1:** Analysis – extending the answer with evaluation or significance.

This structure isn't a writing frame. It's a shared language across our department. Students know what each stage means, and they know what we're looking for. We've also embedded this into our feedback process so that it becomes a living part of how students reflect and improve.

The power of this approach isn't just in the writing – it's in the feedback. We mark to the criteria. We redraft to the criteria. And over time, students begin to internalise it.

HACK #5

The middle step – feedback that drives learning: We talked about the middle step at ResearchEd as one of the biggest game changers in our practice. It's the moment between first draft and final product, where feedback lives.

Again, to reduce the cognitive load which seems to plague students in so many ways, there is a repeated three step format.

- **Read:** Students are given a key list of vocabulary or detail that could be included. Before going any further students are to read through their answer, highlighting both vocabulary and details in the answer, and ticking off on their whole class feedback sheet the details they have included. This has three purposes. Firstly, this gets them to actually read their work before beginning to consider feedback. How often students try to improve a piece of historical writing that they completed three days ago without even looking at what they completed first! Secondly, it allows students to identify and work with complex vocabulary within writing. Finally, it provides an opportunity for students to improve their writing – instead of "death", "execution", for example.

- **Review:** This will be unpicked further but is a middle step as identified by Chiles (2023). This is something that the teacher has identified that the whole class needs to consider before working on their individual targets. It might be a mini reteach if the content isn't secure, potentially looking at some model answers or improving an answer to develop metacognition. The key for this to be successful is for it to be adaptable depending on class, students and task in front of the learners. Often, as part of improving writing skills one step at a time, we use a Build, Better, Best approach. This involves three different model answers of different levels. Students work with these in feedback, highlighting the success criteria, explaining what each answer is doing better than the next, deciding which one their answer is most like. All key strategies to improve student metacognition.
- **Reapply:** This is an opportunity for students to improve their work. This could be practising a different question with the same knowledge, some personalised questions depending on target. Often, this isn't given enough time in lessons. It's essential that students can have opportunities to work independently to improve their targets.

HACK #6

Personalised targets and adaptive scaffolds: Scaffolding isn't one-size-fits-all. Students need different things at different times. The more confident and fluent our students become, the more we can adapt and personalise.

In practice

We use crib sheets, targeted questioning, tiered tasks and structured interventions to ensure support is specific to the student in front of us. This is where formative assessment becomes crucial. Think about the power of:

- Exit tickets that identify misconceptions.
- Seating plans that facilitate peer support.
- QR codes linking to revision videos or task-specific resources.

Personalised scaffolding sends a powerful message to students: "We see where you are, and we believe you can get further."

These are individual to students' targets and link to their success criteria. If a student needs to improve on Success Criteria 2, specific detail, they will be given tasks and questions aiming at this. This allows that personalised target-driven approach based on common misconceptions that students face at each level of the success criteria.

 **HACK #7**

Close the gaps and plan forward: The final piece of scaffolding is what comes next.

- What gaps did your feedback reveal?
- What misconceptions need clearing?
- What knowledge needs to be re-secured before moving on?

We've built this into our planning cycles. Post-assessment doesn't mean moving forward immediately – it means revisiting, rebuilding and refocusing. This helps ensure that progress isn't surface-level.

Sometimes this means reteaching. Other times, it's embedding further retrieval practice into Do Nows, or giving students second attempts. The key is making gap-closing part of your habit, not just a nice-to-have.

Final thought

Scaffolding isn't about making things easier. It's about making success possible. It's the bridge between confusion and clarity, between surface answers and deep understanding.

As we shared at ResearchEd Warrington, the goal isn't to eliminate challenge. It's to structure it. To build the steps that help every student rise to the occasion. And to do it in a way that values the process, not just the outcome.

Because when scaffolding is built in, rather than bolted on, students don't just perform better – they understand better. They develop the confidence and independence to work through challenges and explain their thinking with clarity.

And as teachers, when we see that shift – when students go from passive learners to confident, curious thinkers – that's when we know the scaffold has done its job.

CASE STUDY: KYLE GRAHAM – SCHOLARSHIP

Essentially, scholarship refers to the work of any published historian, or "scholar".

Would you teach science without referring to scientists? No, of course not! However, in history we often teach without referring to the work of the historians who help us to understand the past. Teaching about scholarship and historians helps to make our history curriculum more academic and more accurate. We may not use it in all our lessons in history, but it should be in the majority of them.

How can you do this?

- **Step 1 – audit:** Look at your curriculum. How many historians are referred to within your curriculum? Are they all of a certain demographic? How can you ensure a more diverse range of voices are heard and listened to? Look at the works of Miranda Kauffman when studying The Tudors, or at David Olusoga when studying Empire or World War I.
- **Step 2 – base in scholarship:** Review your current curriculum. You should have an enquiry question about each and every unit. Can that enquiry question be based around a quote from a historian? You don't have to do this, as it may be more prudent to ask something more general, but there is certainly a rationale around basing your enquiry questions, and so your schemes of work, on the efforts of published historians.

- **Step 3 – revisit scholarship regularly:** Scholarship may not form the basis of all of your lessons in a scheme of work, but it should feature regularly. I like to ensure that the view of a historian tops and tails lessons to give students something to base their learning on.

How does this look in lessons?

- **Top and tail – the top:** After the starter activity, introduce a short and snappy view from a historian on the topic you are about to teach. Ask students what the historian may mean by this quote. What does that tell us about the topic we are learning about today?
- **Top and tail – the tail:** Towards the end of the lesson, examine again the views of the historian you have looked at previously. Why might they have come to this conclusion based upon what we have looked at today? How far do we agree with what the historian is saying? For the latter question, it's important to recognise that they are potentially challenging the view of a historian who has spent years or even decades studying something and will have been privy to a lot more information than the students have. We have to take that into account when asking students how far they agree with what the historian is saying.
- **Constant reflection:** If your scheme of learning is based upon a view or quote from a historian, it is worth reflecting back on that quote regularly as students gather more and more knowledge. They could do this at the end of lessons or the beginning, as part of a retrieval-style activity. For example, "Brain Dump – write down all the evidence that shows the Great Depression 'Put the wind in Hitler's sails' – A.J.P. Taylor."
- **Story, source, scholarship:** Created by Dan Warner-Meanwell (2022), this is an excellent way to structure lessons. You have guided reading to start the learning of a new topic in which they create titles or summaries of each paragraph. Then you introduce students to source material, with accompanying questions. Finally, students use all of that information to engage in scholarship, by reading the views of published historians and answering questions based upon them. This ensures that students engage with scholarship in a structure and meaningful way. See the Story Sources Scholarship site for many examples of this.
- **Opposing views:** Introduce students to two views by historians that seem to contradict each other. You can ask students to identify the main differences in the arguments. Students must then piece together information that supports each viewpoint through any variety of tasks that you would usually use to teach them new knowledge. This is a great task for getting students to build an understanding of opposing views and understanding why they may exist in history. Of course, you

can move on to students choosing which view they think is more accurate towards the end if you believe they have enough understanding to make this judgement effectively.

Scholarship is history on a fundamental level and, as such, should be firmly embedded within our curriculum and classroom routines. We should make sure we use a diverse range of historians, thoughts and views and provide students with opportunities to engage with these at every opportunity. There are many ways to deliver scholarship, but deliver it we should.

Often, the process of identifying and working with scholarship allows us to build a more rigorous curriculum, and improves our own subject knowledge. Due to this, we should get different members of our history teams to take responsibility for scholarship in certain topics and schemes of work. It may not always mean re-writing a scheme of work – it may simply be updating it to ensure that the scheme of work is based on current historical thinking.

CHAPTER 13:
FEEDBACK AND
ASSESSMENT – MOVING
LEARNING FORWARD

Every teacher knows the moment: you've marked thirty essays, scribbled pages of feedback, and wonder – did anyone read it?

Feedback is one of the most powerful tools we have, yet also one of the most misunderstood. Done well, it fuels progress. Done poorly, it becomes noise.

Assessment and feedback aren't add-ons to teaching – they are teaching. They shape every decision we make about what to reteach, what to prioritise, and what to celebrate. As Fletcher-Wood (2021) reminds us, summative assessment tells us what happened; formative assessment helps us understand why. The aim isn't to measure learning, but to move it forward.

When feedback becomes habitual and visible, it transforms classroom culture. Students start expecting it, listening for it, using it. And teachers begin to see assessment not as a bureaucratic hoop but as a feedback loop – evidence that drives growth.

HACK #1

Feedback as dialogue, not monologue: "If feedback falls in a classroom and no one hears it, did it make a sound?"

That question always makes me smile because it captures the problem perfectly. We often tell students what to do differently but forget to build the conditions for them to actually do it.

In practice

Feedback only works when it's a dialogue. I dedicate lesson time for students to act on it – what we call the "feed-forward" stage. They read, reflect and rewrite.

I call it the middle step: the space between marking and moving on. It's where learning actually happens.

A simple, structured routine helps:

1. Read your feedback and highlight the key target.

2. Review your work: what already meets the target? This can be a whole-class middle step where students work on looking at a class model, completing a task that allows the teacher to address knowledge misconceptions or using premade models. This can vary depending on the task and the key trends that I see while marking.

3. Reapply it immediately to a new paragraph or question. We've taken recently to breaking this into the success criteria target, and having questions to guide students to how they will make improvements next time.

SC3 Targets (start with this if you didn't feel confident in your explanation)	SC4 Targets	SC5 Targets
Berlin Blockade and Airlift • How did the USA respond/ view the event? • How did the USSR respond/ view the event? • How did the world view the event? Did it affect any other countries? **Atomic Bomb** • How did the USA respond/ view the event? • How did the USSR respond/ view the event? • How did the world view the event? Did it affect any other countries? **Marshall Plan/Truman Doctrine** • How did the USA respond/ view the event? • How did the USSR respond/ view the event? • How did the world view the event? Did it affect any other countries? **Move on to SC4.**	You are continuing to work on your SC4 judgement, but with the 1950s. As with the table we completed, which event from the two was the most important cause of tension? Choose the event that is more important and explain why. • Korean War or Treaty of Friendship. • Treaty of Friendship or NATO/Warsaw Pact. • Korean War or Hungarian Uprising. • Arms and Space Race or Vietnam War. • Vietnam War or NATO/ Warsaw Pact. • Hungarian Uprising or Arms/ Space Race. **Move on to SC5.**	Same knowledge, different skill Write an account of how events from 1947 to 1949 increased Cold War hostilities. (8 marks) Steps to success Paragraph 1 SC1 – Dynamic Opening Sentence: This should answer the question in a sentence and start with "_____ affected Cold War tension, as…" • How did the first event affect the Cold War? SC2 – SPED: Describe what happened in the event. using as much detail as possible. Start with "This was when…" • Key piece of SPED 1. • Key piece of SPED 2. • Key piece of SPED 3. **(as a minimum)** SC3 – Explanation: "This meant that..." • How did the USA respond? • How did the USSR respond? • Did it affect global conflict or any other countries? SC4 – Analysis • Did the event lead to anything else? • Chronology. **Repeat for P2.**

Sometimes we even make this visible: a "feedback carousel" where students rotate and explain how they've applied their target. It builds metacognition and accountability.

The theory

The Education Endowment Foundation (EEF, 2021) notes that feedback focused on action rather than judgement produces greater gains, especially for disadvantaged learners. Students must be taught how to use feedback – not just receive it.

 # HACK #2

Crib sheets – feedback at scale, not at speed: Traditional marking can feel like firefighting – individual, reactive, exhausting. Crib sheet feedback replaces that with precision and pattern-spotting.

In practice

After marking a set of essays, I note the most common strengths and misconceptions. Then, rather than writing the same comment thirty times, I create a one-page crib sheet that:

- Highlights whole-class trends.
- Celebrates best examples ("What a good one looks like").
- Targets key areas for improvement with model sentences.
- Includes a reflection box for students to set a next step.

We use lesson time to unpack it together. Students annotate exemplars, apply corrections and practise improvements immediately. Individual marking becomes coaching, not correcting.

It's efficient, but it's not about cutting corners. It's about maximising impact per minute.

One student told me, "Miss, I prefer crib feedback because I know I'm not the only one who found it hard." That shared experience turns marking into learning.

The theory

The idea of desirable difficulties (Bjork, R. and Bjork, E., 2011) underpins this: deep learning comes from challenge, not ease. The crib approach ensures every student faces the same cognitive lift – analysing, not just absorbing.

HACK #3

Feed forward – close the loop: Feedback without follow-up is wasted effort. The feed-forward cycle ensures that assessment drives progress, not paperwork.

In practice

Our department uses a rhythm that builds this in deliberately. After each formal assessment:

- Week 6: students complete the task.
- Week 7: we reteach based on the patterns revealed.

I plan a Gap Week around those patterns:

- Small-group reteach for recurring misconceptions.
- Mini Do Nows for missed retrieval.
- Short model-building sessions for extended writing issues.

Students see feedback not as punishment but as part of the process.

We also colour-code targets so students can track growth: amber → green → blue. They can literally see their feedback turning into progress over time.

The theory

Black and Wiliam's Assessment for Learning principle (1998) still holds: feedback has no power until it changes teaching. The teacher's response to the evidence – not the marking itself – is what moves learning forward.

 # HACK #4

Make feedback granular and receptive: The best feedback is granular (specific and bite-sized) and receptive (students are emotionally ready to act on it).

In practice

When I return work, I start with three simple statements on the board:

1. What we did well – "Many of you are nailing Success Criteria 2: clear evidence and SPED detail."
2. What to fix next – "Next step: link evidence to impact – Success Criteria 3."
3. What to think about – "How does context shape that argument?"

Students write a short reflection before editing: "My next target is..." followed by an improved example. We call these purple pen moments – visible thinking time.

It's also important to make feedback emotionally safe. I always frame it as belief: "I'm giving you this because I know you can do it." Students internalise that positivity and start to see feedback as investment, not criticism.

The theory

Metacognitive feedback (EEF, 2018) helps students regulate improvement. When combined with self-assessment, it doubles impact because students start anticipating the feedback they'll receive.

 # HACK #5

Use models and WAGOLLs to build confidence: Students can't hit a target they can't see. WAGOLLs make quality visible and achievable.

In practice

Before applying feedback, we dissect exemplar paragraphs. We label structural moves, evidence integration and analytical phrasing. Then students "upgrade" their own work using what they've noticed.

Sometimes I choose an anonymous piece from the class and project it. We work together to strengthen it, narrating decisions: "Let's tighten the causal link here – what phrase could we use instead of 'this shows'?" It turns editing into a collective craft lesson. When students then reattempt their work, the improvement is visible, immediate, and theirs.

The theory
Rosenshine (2012) highlights modelling and guided practice as key to mastery. Feedback lands when it's paired with clear exemplification.

 # HACK #6

Precision, practice, and progress: Effective feedback isn't about more comments – it's about clearer ones and time to act.

In practice
We use the 4R routine from the induction slides:

1. Read the target.
2. Review how it fits the success criteria.
3. Reapply it to a new question.
4. Reach by transferring the skill elsewhere.

This routine makes reflection a habit, not a one-off. Students begin anticipating feedback patterns – "I need to develop SC3 again." That's the moment you know feedback is embedded in their thinking.

The theory
According to Hattie and Timperley (2007), feedback's power lies in its direction: Where am I going? How am I going? Where to next? The 4R cycle operationalises those three questions.

 # HACK #7

Live feedback and whole-class marking: Sometimes the most powerful feedback happens in the moment.

In practice
- During extended writing, I circulate with a clipboard and make live notes: "Three students are missing context. Half are over-describing."
- We pause for two minutes. I model one live fix on the board.
- No marking load later, no delay.
- At the end, I photograph exemplar paragraphs and upload them to the class platform. Students compare their own and self-assess before submission.

This form of real-time formative assessment keeps workload low and responsiveness high.

The theory
Wiliam (2016) describes this as "minute-to-minute assessment." Every adjustment in real time steers learning faster than delayed marking ever could.

HACK #8

Make assessment part of teaching, not after it: Assessment should feel like a natural part of learning, not an interruption.

In practice
I weave short "checkpoints" into each enquiry – a 10-minute write, a paired peer review or a quick self-mark against criteria. Students see that assessment isn't a bolt-on, it's woven through every topic.

By embedding small formative tasks, the final summative piece becomes less intimidating and more diagnostic. The teacher gathers evidence continuously, not retrospectively.

This also supports teacher workload. Instead of marathon marking sessions, you make lots of small, purposeful observations throughout the sequence.

The theory
Fletcher-Wood (2018) defines formative assessment as "noticing learning in progress and responding deliberately." The most effective teachers make that noticing habitual.

HACK #9

Culture first, marking second: Ultimately, feedback thrives in the right culture. Students must believe that improvement is normal, that effort leads to growth and that mistakes are data, not drama.

In practice
- We celebrate re-drafts and resilience. I explicitly praise "best second attempts."
- Every so often, I display side-by-side examples – a before-and-after paragraph from a student who took feedback seriously. It normalises progress as process.
- As a department, we also model that mindset ourselves. We review assessments together, share marking loads and talk openly about what didn't work. Feedback culture starts with teacher collaboration.

The theory

Dweck's growth mindset research (2006) isn't about slogans on walls: it's about systems that reward iteration. When feedback loops are public and shared, improvement becomes part of the identity of the classroom.

Final thought

Assessment and feedback are not the end of learning – they are learning. They're how we listen to our students' thinking, and how we help them listen to themselves.

When feedback is clear, timely, and built into the rhythm of teaching, it stops being a burden and starts being the heartbeat of the classroom. The best feedback doesn't just tell students how they did – it helps them see who they're becoming.

And for teachers, it's liberating: less marking for marking's sake, more meaning. Doing less, better – and seeing learning move forward.

CHAPTER 14: WORKLOAD AND SUSTAINABILITY – DOING LESS, BETTER

There's a running joke in teaching that if you ever start to feel caught up, check your email – it'll pass. Workload is the monster that never quite sleeps. Yet teaching is also a job built on generosity: we give time, energy and emotion freely because we care. The challenge is how to sustain that generosity without burning out.

Early in my career, I thought being a "good" teacher meant being the last car in the car park. I wore exhaustion like a badge of honour. It took me years to realise that being effective isn't the same as being endless. The best teachers I've worked with aren't those who do everything – they're the ones who do enough of the right things well.

HACK #1

Set boundaries without guilt: Boundaries aren't selfish, they're professional.

It's okay to close the laptop. The marking pile can wait. Your students need you rested more than they need you rushed.

In practice

- Use department templates and shared resources. Don't reinvent the wheel unless it's rolling badly.
- Batch mark and timebox tasks – two minutes per essay paragraph can still yield specific, powerful feedback.
- Communicate clearly with colleagues about deadlines. "I can do that, but not this week," is a professional sentence.

The theory

The DfE (2025) stresses that collaborative resource sharing and prioritising impact over perfection reduce burnout without harming learning.

HACK #2

Audit, adapt, abandon: Every term, review your routines. Some will serve you well; others outgrow their usefulness.

In practice

List your top five recurring tasks. For each, ask:

- Does this directly impact student learning?
- Could it be simplified or shared?
- Could it be dropped altogether?

We once stopped double-marking assessments and instead focused on whole-class crib feedback. The world didn't end. In fact, learning improved.

The theory

Tom Sherrington's idea of "high-leverage teaching" applies here – identify the 20% of practices that drive 80% of progress.

HACK #3

Protect planning time: Teaching history requires thought – big-picture curriculum thinking, not just PowerPoint prep. Guard your planning time fiercely.

In practice

- Block out one weekly "curriculum hour." Use it for reading, refining enquiries or discussing pedagogy with colleagues.
- If you can, synchronise departmental PPA. Thinking together is often more efficient than slogging alone.
- Revisit one topic each term and upgrade it, rather than constantly rewriting everything.

Quality planning is an investment that saves hours later.

HACK #4

Use routines to reduce cognitive load: A predictable classroom frees both teacher and students to focus on learning.

In practice
- Consistent lesson structures (Do Now, model, practise, reflect) mean less re-explaining.
- Reusable slide templates, timers and retrieval routines make preparation quicker.
- When students know what to expect, transitions are smooth and focus improves.

The theory
Cognitive load theory (Sweller, 1988) reminds us that mental energy is finite. Routine conserves it for where it matters: explanation, questioning, connection.

HACK #5

Remember the human: Behind every to-do list is a person. Rest is not indulgence; it's maintenance.

Teaching history is emotionally rich work – we deal in stories of humanity, tragedy, courage and change. You can't do that well if you're running on fumes.

Take walks, laugh with colleagues, switch off occasionally. The best resource your students have is a teacher who's still smiling in July.

Final thought
Sustainability isn't about doing less because you care less – it's about doing less because you care enough to last.

If we want our students to love history for life, we need teachers who can teach it for life.

CHAPTER 15: TECHNOLOGY IN HISTORY – USING TOOLS TO ENHANCE, NOT DISTRACT

Technology in education often feels like fashion – everyone's talking about it, and half of it doesn't fit.

Used wisely, tech can amplify learning. Used poorly, it just amplifies noise. The trick is remembering that digital tools are servants, not masters.

When I first started using tech, I equated innovation with impact. Interactive quizzes! Digital timelines! Animated maps! It took a few years to learn that more features didn't mean more learning. The best use of tech is invisible – when students are thinking about history, not the platform.

HACK #1

Use tech to clarify, not complicate: If a digital tool doesn't make learning clearer, it's clutter.

In practice
- Use collaborative documents for joint source analysis – everyone annotates, everyone sees.
- Interactive timelines help visualise causation and continuity.
- Digital polling tools like Mentimeter or Forms quickly surface misconceptions in real time.

Ask yourself: Would this task be better on paper? If the answer's yes, it belongs on paper.

The theory
EEF's digital technology guidance report (2021) stresses that tech improves outcomes only when tightly aligned to pedagogy, not novelty.

HACK #2

Retrieval goes digital: Tech excels at repetition and feedback – perfect for retrieval practice.

In practice
- Create quick quizzes using Quizizz, Kahoot or Google Forms to reinforce chronology or definitions.
- Set "two-minute history recalls" at the start of lessons. Students enjoy the gamified format, and instant results reveal class gaps.
- Then, crucially, discuss the answers aloud – the learning isn't in the quiz, it's in the conversation after.

HACK #3

Bring the past to life: Technology can bridge classroom walls, letting students see, hear and explore history beyond the textbook.

In practice
- Virtual museum tours (e.g., British Museum, Imperial War Museum).
- Archival video clips and oral histories from BFI or BBC archives.
- Interactive maps of empire, trade routes or migration.

These resources give students a sensory connection to the past, sparking curiosity and empathy.

But avoid the trap of "click tourism" – guide their attention with purposeful questions. "What do you notice?" "What surprised you?"

HACK #4

Digital literacy is historical literacy: Students today encounter history daily – through TikTok timelines, memes and YouTube commentary. Teaching them to evaluate those interpretations is part of our job.

In practice

Use examples of online history content – a tweet, a video, an infographic – and ask:

- Who made this?
- What's their purpose?
- What evidence is used?

This helps students apply the same source skills digitally that we teach academically.

The theory

Wineburg (2018) argues that the challenge of the digital age isn't access to information but discernment – knowing what to trust.

Final thought

Technology doesn't replace great teaching; it amplifies it. Used wisely, it saves time, engages students and extends reach. Used thoughtlessly, it drains time and attention. Enhance, don't distract – that's the historian's rule of thumb.

CHAPTER 16: ADVICE FOR EARLY CAREER TEACHERS – BUILDING CONFIDENCE, CRAFT AND CLASSROOM PRESENCE

Every teacher remembers their first term: juggling behaviour, marking and the fear that someone will realise you're making it up as you go. The truth is, we all are to some extent.

Teaching history well takes time. It's not just about delivering content but developing craft – that blend of explanation, questioning and empathy that turns lessons into learning.

HACK #1

Focus on core routines: Don't try to do everything brilliantly – do a few things consistently.

In practice

- Perfect your lesson openings: calm starts, clear expectations, retrieval warm-ups.
- Rehearse transitions and instructions out loud.
- Use simple, repeated phrasing: "Pens down. Eyes up. Let's recap."

Routines build confidence. They create space for your personality to shine once structure holds firm.

HACK #2

Teach, then reflect, then tweak: No lesson will ever be perfect, and that's fine.

After each one, jot a quick note: What worked? What will I change next time? Small refinements over time build craft faster than chasing perfection.

Observation can be powerful if you watch for craft, not performance. Ask colleagues, "How do you get students to..." rather than "Can you give me a resource?" You'll learn much more.

HACK #3

Know your subject deeply: Subject knowledge is your safety net. The deeper you understand it, the freer you are to teach creatively.

In practice

- Read beyond the specification – *BBC History Extra*, *History Today*, podcasts like *You're Dead to Me*.
- Keep a "subject CPD" folder: key dates, misconceptions, new interpretations.
- Talk history with your department – they're your best resource.

Students can tell when you love your subject. Enthusiasm is contagious.

HACK #4

Manage the emotional load: Teaching drains energy as well as time. Protect both.

Find mentors who listen, not just advise. Celebrate small wins: a well-managed discussion, a tricky class that finally engaged.

Remember – consistency beats charisma. Presence grows with confidence, and confidence grows with practice.

HACK #5

Keep perspective: You will make mistakes. Every teacher does. The difference between surviving and thriving is reflection.

As one mentor told me, "You don't need to be the best teacher in the room – you just need to get a little better every week."

The theory

According to Ingersoll (2012), early-career retention correlates with mentorship and manageable workload. Surround yourself with people who remind you you're learning too.

Final thought

Teaching history is not about being perfect. It's about being purposeful.

Trust that you'll grow, and remember – every "hack" in this book began as someone's mistake, refined over time. Yours will too.

CHAPTER 17: STUDENT VOICE AND AGENCY – EMPOWERING THE LEARNERS OF HISTORY

One of the best moments in teaching is when students start challenging you – politely, insightfully and with evidence. That's when you know they're becoming historians.

Student voice isn't about handing over control of the classroom. It's about giving students a genuine stake in their learning. When they feel heard, they engage more deeply – not because they're being entertained, but because they're being respected. These little actions aren't day to day, but making students feel heard in the classroom means that they can see the purpose clearer, even little things in the build up to an assessment: "What would we like to revise?" "Hands up for...". This allows some autonomy for students and ensures that lessons can be effectively tailored to meet the needs of the students.

HACK #1

Ask, don't assume: We often design lessons for students without asking them. Simple feedback routines – "Which part of this topic helped you understand most?" – can reshape teaching quickly.

In practice
After each unit, I run a short "history review":

- "What's one thing that helped you learn?"
- "What's one thing that confused you?"
- "What would you like to explore next?"

Patterns emerge. Sometimes they confirm what we thought, sometimes they surprise us. Either way, students see that their voice matters.

HACK #2

Build ownership through enquiry: Students thrive when they drive the questions.

In practice
In the final lesson of a topic, ask students to design the next enquiry: "If you could investigate one question from this era, what would it be?"

Display their questions, then use one or two in future sequences. When they spot their question on the board weeks later, the pride is palpable.

This doesn't mean abandoning rigour – it means weaving curiosity into structure.

HACK #3

Encourage debate, not just discussion: Voice also means argument – respectful, evidence-based, historically grounded.

In practice
- Run mini history seminars. Give students a provocative question, e.g., "Was the Industrial Revolution progress or pain?"
- Use talk tokens or structured turn-taking.
- Students learn to listen, challenge and justify.

These debates teach citizenship as much as history – students practise disagreeing well.

 **HACK #4**

Construct success together: Involve students in defining what "good" looks like.

In practice

Before an assessment, share a model answer. Ask:

- "What makes this effective?"
- "What's missing?"

Build a class success criteria list together. Ownership of the rubric builds understanding – it's feedback before feedback.

 HACK #5

Celebrate contribution, not just compliance: Agency grows through recognition. Celebrate thoughtful questions, curiosity and perseverance as much as grades.

Showcase student projects, essays, or oral histories on corridor displays. Host a Historian of the Month. When students see their voices reflected, they begin to see themselves as historians.

Final thought

Empowering students doesn't mean letting go of authority; it means redefining it.

In the best history classrooms, power isn't lost – it's shared. Students don't just learn history – they help make it.

CONCLUSION

The craft, the chaos and the joy of teaching history

There's something about teaching history that gets under your skin. Maybe it's the stories, maybe it's the debates, maybe it's the way one minute you're explaining the Treaty of Versailles and the next you're fielding a Year 8 question about whether you'd survive in medieval England ("Miss, you'd definitely die first"). Whatever it is, it's a subject that demands both heart and craft – and a healthy sense of humour.

Writing this book has reminded me that being a history teacher is a strange mix of juggling act, marathon and art form. You're constantly balancing knowledge and curiosity, structure and freedom, exam board demands and your own desire to make students love the subject as much as you do.

And yet, for all its challenges, there is something magical about it.

There's the moment a Year 7 finally sees how the Norman Conquest links to Parliament, or when a Year 11 student uses the word "significance" perfectly in an essay and looks just as proud as you feel. There's the quiet buzz in the classroom when students are mid-debate, voices rising, ideas forming. And there's the best part – when a student who "hated history" in September tells you in July that it's their favourite subject.

That's the heartbeat of what we do.

The big picture

If you've made it to this chapter, you'll know that the "hacks" in this book were never really about shortcuts. They're about thoughtfulness. About using what we know from research, theory and experience to make classroom life a little easier, a little more purposeful and a lot more joyful.

Teaching history isn't a checklist. It's a craft, one that we get better at by reflecting, refining and learning from each other.

Over the years, I've learned that curriculum design isn't about cramming everything in – it's about knowing what not to include. Questioning isn't about being clever – it's about being curious. Source analysis isn't about ticking AO3 boxes – it's about giving students the confidence to interrogate ideas. Writing isn't about structure – it's about voice and argument.

And, perhaps most importantly, history teaching isn't about us performing knowledge – it's about helping students build it.

As Counsell (2018) reminds us, curriculum is "an argument about the world." Every topic we teach is a choice, and every choice shapes how our students understand themselves and others. That's a privilege – and a responsibility.

Finding your balance

It's easy to feel overwhelmed by everything we're supposed to do. To juggle marking, data, pastoral work and parents' evenings, and still find time to plan coherent, evidence-informed lessons.

But I've learned to find peace in the idea that we'll never get it all perfect – and that's okay.

Some lessons will soar. Others will stumble. One class will grasp causation beautifully, another will forget who won the English Civil War (again). But each misstep teaches us something, each tweak makes the next lesson stronger.

The best history teachers I know aren't the ones with the neatest displays or the most elaborate PowerPoints. They're the ones who love their subject, think deeply about it and never stop trying to make it clearer, fairer and more meaningful for their students.

As Wiliam (2011) puts it, "Every teacher needs to improve, not because they are not good enough, but because they can be even better."

The history teacher's toolkit

If you were to strip this book down to its core message, it would be this: Good history teaching rests on three things – clarity, connection and curiosity.

- **Clarity:** Helping students know where they are in the story, why it matters and how it connects to what came before.
- **Connection:** Building bridges between topics, ideas and people so students can see the big picture of the past.
- **Curiosity:** Making students want to know more – not because it's on the exam, but because they're genuinely fascinated.

And all of that happens in the small, ordinary moments: the Do Now that sparks a link to a previous topic, the questioning sequence that teases out a misconception, the modelling that shows students how historians think.

It's the little things that turn lessons into learning.

When the plane is mid-flight

At the start of the book, I compared teaching history to trying to fix a plane while it's mid-flight. I still think that's about right. The job never really stops. The curriculum keeps changing, new research keeps emerging and your Year 10s keep forgetting how to structure a paragraph.

But that's the beauty of it.

Because history is about change – and so is teaching. We adapt, we adjust, we evolve. We keep asking, "What worked? What didn't? What's next?" We keep learning.

Sometimes, when I'm knee-deep in exam prep or trying to design another retrieval quiz, I remind myself: this job matters. Not just because we're teaching history, but because we're teaching students to think historically – to weigh evidence, challenge assumptions and see the world in context.

In a world of instant answers and polarised opinions, that might be one of the most important things we can do.

The real hack

If you take one thing from this book, I hope it's this: There's no single "hack" that will transform your teaching overnight.

But there are hundreds of small, smart, compassionate choices that can transform how your students learn.

Keep reflecting. Keep talking to colleagues. Keep stealing great ideas. Keep trying something new, even if it flops the first time.

And never forget that what we do is extraordinary.

We teach the stories of humanity – its triumphs, its mistakes, its courage, its cruelty. We help students understand that the past isn't gone, it's living all around them. And in doing that, we help them write the next part of that story with more empathy, understanding, and perspective.

That's what makes it worth it.

Final words

So here's to you – the history teachers who plan late, mark endlessly and somehow still find the energy to make the Peasants' Revolt sound exciting on a rainy Friday afternoon.

Here's to the quiet wins – the student who finally uses a Tier 3 word correctly, the one who surprises you with a brilliant question, the class that debates for ten whole minutes without you needing to intervene.

And here's to the joy – because for all the chaos, the deadlines and the endless cups of coffee, there's nothing quite like watching young people learn to see the world through the lens of history.

We are the storytellers, the scaffolders, the questioners, the keepers of curiosity.

And even on the toughest days, that's something to be proud of.

William Faulkner said, "The past isn't dead. It isn't even past."

Neither, I'd argue, is the work of a history teacher. It lives on – in every question, every conversation, every spark of curiosity we light.

BIBLIOGRAPHY

Alexander, R. (2017). *Towards dialogic teaching: Rethinking classroom talk.* 5th edn. Dialogos.

Ashby, R. and Lee, P. (2000). 'Progression in historical understanding among students ages 7–14'. in P. Stearns, P. Seixas and S. Wineburg (Eds.), *Knowing, teaching, and learning history: National and international perspectives.* New York University Press.

Ausubel, D.P. (1968). *Educational psychology: A cognitive view.* Holt, Rinehart and Winston.

Baddeley, A.D. (2000). 'Short-term and working memory' in Tulving, E. and Craik, F.I.M. (eds.), *The Oxford handbook of memory,* 77–92. Oxford University Press.

Ball, S. J. (2013). *The Education Debate.* Policy Press.

Bandura, A. (1997). Self-efficacy: The exercise of control. W. H. Freeman.

Beck, I.L., McKeown, M.G. and Kucan, L. (2002). Bringing Words to Life: Robust Vocabulary Instruction. Guilford Press.

Berliner, D. (2004). 'Describing the behaviour and documenting the accomplishments of expert teachers.' *Bulletin of Science, Technology and Society,* 24(3), 200–212.

Bishop, R.S. (1990). 'Mirrors, windows, and sliding glass doors'. *Perspectives,* 1(3), ix–xi

Bjork, R.A. and Bjork, E.L. (2011). 'Making things hard on yourself, but in a good way: Creating desirable difficulties to enhance learning'. in M. Gernsbacher *et al.* (Eds.), *Psychology and the real world.* Worth Publishers.

Black, P. and Wiliam, D. (1998). 'Assessment and Classroom Learning'. *Assessment in Education: Principles, Policy and Practice,* 5(1), 7–74.

Brown, P., Roediger, H. and McDaniel, M. (2014). *Make it stick: The science of successful learning.* Harvard University Press.

Bruner, J.S. (1960). *The process of education.* Harvard University Press.

Burn, K. and Harris, R. (2016). 'Historical association report: Teacher knowledge and curriculum coherence'. *Teaching History,* 163, 44–52.

Cepeda N.J., Pashler, H., Vul, E., Wixted, J.T., Rohrer, D. (2006) 'Distributed practice in verbal recall tasks: A review and quantitative synthesis'. *Psychol Bull.* 132(3), 354–80.

Chapman, A. (2011). 'Historical interpretations'. *Teaching History,* 144, 32–41.

Chiles, M. (2023). The feedback pendulum: A manifesto for enhancing feedback in education. John Catt Educational.

Christodoulou, D. (2017). Making good progress? The future of assessment for learning. Oxford University Press.

Coe, R., Aloisi, C., Higgins, S. and Major, L. (2014). *What makes great teaching? Review of the underpinning research.* Sutton Trust.

Collins, M. (2018). 'Teaching historiography in the secondary classroom.' *Teaching History,* 171, 8–15.

Cooper, H. (2017). 'Diversity and coherence in the history curriculum'. *Teaching History*, 166, 18–25.

Counsell, C. (2011). 'Disciplinary knowledge for all: The secondary history curriculum and history teachers' achievement'. *Curriculum Journal*, 22(2), 201–225.

Counsell, C. (2018). 'Taking curriculum seriously'. *Impact*, 4.

Counsell, C. (2020). 'Taking curriculum seriously – Revisited'. *Impact*, 9.

Counsell, C. (2021). 'Curriculum thinking and the quest for coherence'. *Teaching History*, 182, 10–18.

Counsell, C., Burn, K., Fordham, M. and Foster, R. (2016). 'Get excited and carry on'. *Teaching History*, 163:2–2

DfE. (2013). The National Curriculum in England: Framework document. Department for Education.

DfE. (2025). *Reducing school workload*. Department for Education.

Dewey, J. (1938). *Experience and education*. Macmillan.

Didau, D. (2015). What if everything you knew about education was wrong?. Crown House Publishing.

Dignath, C. and Veenman, M.V.-J. (2021). 'The role of self-regulated learning in education: A review'. *Educational Psychology Review*, 33, 1039–1075.

Dweck, C.S. (2006). Mindset: The new psychology of success. Random House.

EEF. (2018). Metacognition and self-regulated learning: Guidance report. EEF.

EEF. (2019). Improving literacy in secondary schools: Guidance report. EEF.

EEF. (2021). Teacher feedback to improve pupil learning: Guidance report. EEF.

EEF. (2021). Using digital technology to improve learning: Guidance report. EEF.

Fletcher-Wood, H. (2018). Responsive teaching: Cognitive science and formative assessment in practice. Routledge.

Fletcher-Wood, H. (2021). Habits of success: Getting every student learning. Routledge.

Fordham, M. (2016). 'Teachers and the academic disciplines'. *Journal of Philosophy of Education*, 50, 419–31.

Hattie, J. (2013). Visible learning: A synthesis of over 800 meta-analyses relating to achievement. Routledge.

Hattie, J. and Timperley, H. (2007). 'The power of deedback'. *Review of Educational Research*, 77(1), 81–112.

Hochman, J.C., Wexler, N. and Lemov, D. (2024). *The writing revolution 2.0: a guide to advanced thinking through writing in all subjects and grades*. Jossey-Bass.

Ingersoll, R.M. (2012). 'Beginning teacher induction: What the data tell us'. *Phi Delta Kappan*, 93(8), 47–51.

Karpicke, J. and Roediger, H. (2008). 'The critical importance of retrieval for learning'. *Science*, 319, 966–8.

Lambert, D. and Biddulph, M. (2015). 'The place of knowledge in the geography curriculum: Towards a "curriculum with purpose"'. *Curriculum Journal*, 26(2), 152–179.

LeCocq, H. (2000) 'Beyond bias: Making source evaluation meaningful to Year 7.' *Teaching History*, 99, 50–55.

Leat, D. (1998) *Thinking through geography*. Chris Kington Publishing.

Lemov, D. (2021). *Teach like a champion 3.0*. Jossey-Bass.

Mercer, N. (2000). *Words and minds: how we use language to think together* (1st ed.). Routledge.

Myatt, M. (2019). *The curriculum: Gallimaufry to coherence*. John Catt Educational.

Perkins, D. (1993). 'Teaching for Understanding'. *American Educator*, 17(3), 28–35.

Piaget, J. (1952). *The origins of intelligence in children*. International Universities Press.

Pintrich, P.R. (2000). 'The role of goal orientation in self-regulated learning'. in M. Boekaerts *et al.* (Eds.), *Handbook of self-regulation*. Academic Press.

Quigley, A. (2018). *Closing the vocabulary gap*. Routledge.

Quigley, A. (2022). *Closing the writing gap*. Routledge.

Rosenshine, B. (2012). 'Principles of instruction: Research-based strategies that all teachers should know'. *American Educator*, 36(1), 12–19.

Rowe, M.B. (1974), 'Reflections on wait-time: Some methodological questions'. *J. Res. Sci. Teach.*, 11, 263–279.

Ryan, R.M. and Deci, E.L. (2000). 'Self-determination theory and the facilitation of intrinsic motivation, social development, and well-being'. *American Psychologist*, 55(1), 68–78.

Seixas, P. (2006). *Benchmarks of historical thinking: A framework for assessment in Canada*. Centre for the Study of Historical Consciousness. UBC.

Seixas, P. and Morton, T. (2013). *The big six historical thinking concepts*. Nelson Education.

Sherrington, T. (2019). *Rosenshine's principles in action*. John Catt Educational.

Sweller, J. (1988). 'Cognitive load during problem solving: Effects on learning'. *Cognitive Science*, 12(2), 257–285.

Vygotsky, L.S. (1978). Mind in society: The development of higher psychological processes. Harvard University Press.

Warner-Meanwell, D. (2022). *Story, Source, Scholarship*.

A collaborative resource for History teachers.

Wiggins, G. and McTighe, J. (2005). *Understanding by design*. 2nd edn.. ASCD.

Wiliam, D. (2011). *Embedded formative assessment*. Solution Tree Press.

Wiliam, D. (2018). Creating the schools our children need: Why what we're doing now won't help much (and what we can do instead). Learning Sciences International.

Willingham, D.T. (2009). *Why don't students like school?*. Jossey-Bass.

Wiltshire, T. (2000). 'Telling and suggesting in the Conwy Valley'. *Teaching History*, 100, Thinking and Feeling Edition.

Wineburg, S. (2001). Historical thinking and other unnatural acts: Charting the future of teaching the past. Temple University Press.

Wineburg, S. (2018). *Why learn history (when it's already on your phone)*. University of Chicago Press.

Wood, S. (1995). 'Developing an understanding of time – sequencing issues'. *Teaching History*, 79, 11–14

Wrigglesworth, J. and McKeever, M. (2010). 'Writing history: A genre-based, interdisciplinary approach linking disciplines, language and academic skills'. *Arts and Humanities in Higher Education*, 9(1), 107–126.

Young, M. (2014). Knowledge and the future school: Curriculum and the social justice of powerful knowledge. Bloomsbury Academic.

Zimmerman, B.J. and Bandura, A. (1994). 'Impact of self-regulatory influences on writing course achievement'. *American Educational Research Journal*, 31(4), 845–862.